FLAUTAS
PASTOR
ENCHILADAS

Vitamina T

CDMX
ILUMINACIÓ
CERRAMOS LOS SA
Victoria No. 32 Local E, Co
SÓLO
TACOS DE CABEZA

Jorge Gaviria & Fermín Núñez
with Allegra Ben-Amotz

Vitamina T

Your Daily Dose of Tacos, Tortas, Tamales, and More Mexican Street Food Classics

Photographs by Jeni Afuso and Dylan James Ho

Clarkson Potter / Publishers
New York

Tamales

Todo lo Demás / Everything Else

Toques Finales / Final Touches

INTRO

by Jorge Gaviria

"I'm headed to Mexico with some friends next month. Any food recs?" —Everyone

As the chef/co-owner of one of the most acclaimed Mexican restaurants in the United States and the founder of an award-winning Mexican food brand, respectively (more about your hosts of this cookbook collab in a minute), keeping up with requests for our favorite food spots in Mexico has come to feel somewhat like a full-time job.

With growing international interest in all things Mexico, this tracks. The world just can't seem to get enough of Mexican food, and with good reason: It's kind of . . . well, you know . . . the best.

Don't just take our word for it. You needn't look any further than the fact that, for example, as of more than a decade ago, Mexican cuisine had become among the first in the world to be recognized as a UNESCO cultural heritage of humanity. Or, perhaps Mexico's growing representation on the World's 50 Best Restaurants list and recent domination of the prestigious Michelin Guide might mean something to you.

No matter the case, Mexican gastronomy is finally being valued for the global powerhouse it has always been; and it's certainly about time.

Cool, so, how about those recs?

Hang tight. First, a story.

I was in my mid-twenties, moments before birthing a little-known masa start-up called Masienda, and on my first trip to Mexico since childhood.

Like those well-meaning children who fail the marshmallow test, I had already managed to blow my entire life savings as a middle-school-teacher-turned-line-cook eating at some of Mexico City's globally renowned restaurants. At Pujol, I'd finally gotten to taste the revelation that is "mole madre" (its famous mole, continuously cooked for months . . . clocking in at roughly 327 days old the night I tried it for myself). There were then escamoles at Máximo Bistrot, sopa seca de natas at Nicos, everything but the kitchen sink at Azul Histórico, not one but two tasting menus at Quintonil, and a lifetime's worth of guayaba rolls at Panadería Rosetta.

Okay, so maybe I was riding dirty into credit-card debt by the time that trip ended, but no matter, I digress.

As memorable as each of these experiences decidedly was, it was the full-body high I encountered at one stop in particular that I still find myself chasing to this very day. Walking between restaurant meals, in a residential neighborhood I still couldn't confidently place on a map if I tried, I stumbled upon a tianguis, or open-air market, made up entirely of makeshift food stalls. It was still comida (lunchtime), and every single puesto that met the eye was buzzing with discerning customers. Some people were sitting on neon plastic stools with disposable plates on their laps while others stood, heads tilted to the side, professionally putting away some of the most delicious-looking foods I'd ever laid eyes on: hand-pressed corn tortillas topped with flossy, glistening pork carnitas; fava-filled blue corn tlacoyos studded with a green mountain of chopped nopales; tostadas smothered in refried beans and queso fresco; tamales de elote with hot atole; and on, and on, and on.

Naturally, with several hours and a handful of kilometers left between me and my next reservation, I ate my way through nearly every stall I could, being sure to not repeat a single dish among them. As it happened, each bite was impossibly more exquisite than the one that preceded it, and—wouldn't you know?—this dining experience managed to transcend those I'd cherry-picked from my favorite restaurant guides.

Sometime just before tapping out, I walked past the taco stall at which I'd begun my crawl, this time with a tlacoyo in hand, and I happened to catch the eye of the taquero who had served me earlier.

"You found it!" he said in Spanish.

I looked down at my tlacoyo and back up at him, worried I'd offended him somehow by eating someone else's creation within his eyeshot. "The tlacoyo?" I asked.

"Vitamina T. You found it!" he repeated with a big smile. "Now you know where to find us for your next dose—we'll be here waiting!"

Surveying the 100+ recipes that make up *Vitamina T*, it is easy to appreciate what makes this playful term for Mexico's standout street food so deeply tantalizing: the sizzling sounds and seductive smells of a late-night taqueria, a metric kilo of pure torta magic, a charcoal-burning clay comal teeming with tetelas wrapped in hoja santa leaves, and all of the tamales, all of the time. These dishes, which all happen to start with the letter *T*, are emblematic of what makes Mexico a culinary superpower. They are among the very greatest of the greatest hits, and as even the most famous Mexican chefs in the world would likely agree, they're best represented far outside the luxurious confines of fine dining.

Vitamina T makes for some of the most spectacular experiences in Mexico and also some of its most elusive. Seeking out tianguis like the one I stumbled upon can sometimes feel like tracking down the wish-granting Zoltar machine at a traveling carnival: They're here one moment and gone the next. They are seemingly open only on the second Tuesday of the third month of the lunar year, unless that Tuesday falls on a holiday, in which case it'll just skip to the following Wednesday.

It is true that my taquero friend may indeed "be waiting" for me, but so is the reality that I'll never know exactly where or when to find him again. And so it sometimes goes when it comes to the transient nature of street food: We have to get it while it's hot.

Or . . . we could just make it ourselves.

[Cue Fermín, enters stage right.] It is on this note that I proudly introduce to you my dear friend, *Vitamina T* wellness coach, recipe writer, and spirit partner for this cookbook, Fermín Núñez. Fermín is the chef and co-owner of Austin's beloved Suerte and Este restaurants. If you haven't had the pleasure of enjoying his smashing Suadero Tacos with Black Magic Oil in person, you may have perhaps seen his work featured in *Bon Appétit*, *The Wall Street Journal*, Munchies, or Netflix's hit show *Taco Chronicles*. Born and raised in Coahuila, a northern state of Mexico that borders South Texas, Fermín quite literally grew up at the intersection where Mexican and American cultures collide. At his restaurants, Fermín's cooking is as much a testament to his laid-back vibe as it is to this lived duality: an exploration of local and global flavors and ingredients, traditional and unconventional techniques—all with the grounded, unwavering presence of freshly milled masa and [*clutches rosary*] the occasional flour tortilla for good measure.

Of course, where there's fresh masa, vitamina T surely follows. In fact, when Suerte opened, it had an entire menu section named for masa, filled with some of my favorites, like squash tetelas and mushroom tlayudas. (I guess Zoltar has his own way of finding you again when you least expect it.) Needless to say, from the very first moment I visited the restaurant, I was hooked—so much so that from that meal on, I found myself exploring just about any which way we could start working together, from the short film series that earned Masienda its first James Beard Award, to some of my all-time favorite recipe videos, and eventually, to this book.

To quote Fermín, "You can't produce the remix without first sampling the classics." To this end, we both wanted to see a cookbook in the world that organized our favorite Mexican street-food formats by chapter, each with a strong foundation of regional, time-tested chart toppers mixed with some deeper cuts and fresh pop numbers peppered throughout. In other words, this book is designed to be one of the greatest recipe mixtapes of all time that we know you'll be cooking from for years to come.

Oh, yes, I almost forgot. About those recs! This is less a guidebook for where to eat in Mexico than it is a compass for what to eat and how to prepare it at home. To be sure, we will include a few Easter eggs for good measure, but by the end of this cookbook, our hope is that you will feel empowered to identify what you love most about this soul-satisfying cuisine and continue to explore it for yourself, both in and out of your kitchen.

Ven a comer, friends.

Whether it is your first time cooking Mexican food at home (welcome!) or you are the executive "jeff" of your very own Mexican restaurant (welcome!), the following tools and ingredients will be referenced throughout this cookbook. While not every single line item is mission-critical for reaching the vitamina T flow state (e.g., stand mixer), they can make your life easier, and we will nevertheless provide you with some context as to why or how we might use them. On that note: Jorge is the founder and part-owner of Masienda, as well as an author of this book, but this is not a Masienda cookbook, if you know what we mean. We will occasionally recommend products that Masienda sells, because we, and a large community of chefs and home cooks, believe in their quality, but the choice will always be yours.

Tools

Blender: We use them. Especially if we are short on time while making large batches of Salsa Taquera (page 246) or are cooking at the in-laws' house sans molcajete. Any blender will do, but we are partial to Vitamix blenders, both personally and professionally, and were not paid to say so. Like James Brown, they are the hardest-working blenders in the business and, like Sade, the smoothest of operators—real nice-sounding, too. Pro tip: Vitamix's certified reconditioned series delivers the same legacy quality for a fraction of the cost.

Bowls: Lots of bowls for mixing masa, soaking and cleaning chiles, etc.

Comal: A circular-shaped griddle used in Mesoamerican kitchens. It will be referenced throughout this book to denote any kind of nonstick cooking surface—traditional comal or otherwise. We recipe-tested with a range of nonstick pans, including the Made In x Masienda carbon-steel comal.

Digital Scale: We won't be getting surgically precise in most of these recipes, but for baked goods like Vanilla Conchas (page 226), a digital scale makes a big difference.

Dutch Oven: For all low-and-slow cooking, from guisados (braises) to confit, and for an occasional fried application. We personally love the heat retention (and the look) of the Made In Dutch oven series.

Fine-Mesh Sieve: For straining stocks, draining potatoes, and everything in between.

Food Processor: A great hack for a molcajete-textured, chunky salsa or spread like Sikil Pak (page 48), even if it turns out ever-so-slightly less flavorful than a salsa made with a real molcajete.

Hand Mixer: If you do not own a stand mixer, an electric hand mixer will make for lighter work than an old-fashioned whisk and some elbow grease. When using a hand mixer to mix masa for tamales, keep in mind that you may need to work in multiple smaller batches to produce the results of a stand mixer.

Immersion Blender: When you don't have critical mass in a blender container to get a proper blend, immersion blenders are a handy trick.

Latex Gloves: For cleaning all chiles. Just a suggestion, unless you are positive you will remember to wash your hands thoroughly between cleaning chiles and rubbing your eyes.

Molcajete: Ubiquitous in kitchens across Mexico, a molcajete is a mortar and pestle made of fine-grained lava rock used for preparing salsa and guacamole, as well as grinding spices, chiles, and more. It requires a bit more elbow grease than a blender, sure, but we promise it will elevate whatever flavors you fill it with. We are partial to Masienda's molcajete because we personally know the artisans who make them and can vouch for their design and craftsmanship, but any basalt molcajete will do the trick.

Scissors: For cleaning dried chiles.

Sheet Pan (with Wire Rack!): Sheet pans, pretty straightforward; wire racks, perhaps less intuitive for most home cooks. Among a handful of utilitarian functions, wire racks help diffuse and circulate heat from the bottom surface of your metal sheet pan, so your food doesn't overheat—clutch for Baked Tostadas (page 26), roasting (and resting!) a chicken, and draining fried foods.

Spider Strainer: For handling the occasional fried food.

Stand Mixer: There are only a handful of pastry items in this cookbook but almost a dozen tamal recipes whose prep is simplified by a stand mixer. You can definitely get by without using one, but if you are graduating, getting married, or retiring anytime soon, you might consider manifesting one.

Tamal Steamer: Unless you are hosting a proper tamalada (tamal-making party), you don't need to run out to buy a large tamal steamer (tamalera), capable of cooking several dozen tamales at a time. Any kind of steam basket insert will work, provided it fits your existing pot. You can also create a makeshift tamal steamer by bunching up corn husks at the bottom of a pot and stacking your tamales accordingly. We tested our tamal recipes using Made In's stainless steel 8-quart clad stockpot and steam basket, which we loved.

Thermometer: A handful of recipes call for specific temperature readings, such as for cooking chicken or making cheese and for maintaining hot oil when deep-frying. A digital instant-read thermometer is most helpful for general cooking, and a candy/deep-fry thermometer that clips onto the inside of a pot is best for frying oil.

Tortilla Press: Tortillas, tostadas, and tetelas are just a few of the masa (dough) shapes we cover that will benefit from the efficiency and accuracy of a tortilla press. To use a tortilla press, you need to line it with two sheets of plastic, preferably cut from a thin shopping bag or freezer bag. This keeps the masa from sticking to either plate of the press. Masienda sells an award-winning, food-safe tortilla press produced by artisans in Mexico that comes with a premeasured, reusable liner set, for your convenience.

Tortilla Warmer: Tortilla warmers are not just lovely table accessories but also tools specially designed to keep tortillas warm and hold in precious moisture in the form of steam that helps keep a tortilla soft and pliable throughout your meal. The crucial step to making tortillas that are pliable and pillowy rather than dry and crumbly is giving them a final steam after searing. You can use a clean kitchen towel, a woven basket (a.k.a. chiquihuite), or a tortilla warmer or pouch.

Wooden Cutting Board: Nice things are nice, and a thick wooden cutting board is a nice thing to have; it's natural, more forgiving on knives, and Fermín thinks everyone would do well to own one.

Ingredients

Achiote (Annato) Paste: A key ingredient for making adobos and a staple of Yucatecan cooking. Fermín prefers working from the seed (La Boîte brand, especially) instead of the paste, but El Yucateco or El Mexicano are decent options, if you're craving a shortcut.

Avocado Leaf: A relative of bay (laurel) leaves, hojas de aguacate (avocado leaves) are prized for the anise flavor they impart to foods, beans in particular. Available at select Mexican grocers, and usually in stock on Amazon. Keep an eye out for whole-leaf options.

Beans: Your beans are your business, and canned beans are welcome to this party, FWIW. That said, we occasionally reference a few deep cuts like bayo and ayocote beans, which you can find at specialty online purveyors like Masienda and the OG, Rancho Gordo.

Calcium Hydroxide (Cal): A highly basic (i.e., alkaline) powder derived from limestone used for nixtamalizing corn, among other applications.

Cilantro: Don't garnish your tacos without cilantro, unless you have that aversion that means it tastes like soap.

Cinnamon: Whenever we call for cinnamon sticks, we mean Mexican cinnamon, a.k.a. canela, a.k.a. Ceylon.

Dried Chiles: Dried does not necessarily mean *not* fresh. In other words, there is a difference between fresh dried chiles and *stale* dried chiles, and you'll do well to procure the former. When sourcing chiles, try to avoid chiles that are dry to the point of being brittle, cracking, or damaged. We find the bulk chile bins at our neighborhood Mexican grocers to carry the freshest retail inventory because their inventory moves at higher velocities than bagged chiles at conventional grocery stores. Dried chiles are, of course, also available online. We enjoy The Chile Guy's (thechileguy.com) catalog and quality, even if it means buying a little bit extra to hit the one-pound minimum.

In terms of flavor, red dried chiles like guajillo, puya, piquín, morita, chipotle, and árbol tend to have a thinner skin, more acidity, and widely varying spice levels, whereas dark dried chiles like ancho, pasilla, and mulato have a sweeter, raisin-y flavor, chewier texture, and milder heat range. For all recipes that call for dried chiles, we recommend removing their stems with scissors and cutting a slit lengthwise down each chile to remove the seeds, which are bitter in flavor.

When toasting dried chiles, it's generally a good idea to open a window or turn on a fan, as the capsaicin—the spicy component from the chiles—will release into the air.

Store dried chiles in an airtight container away from light and heat, somewhere like your pantry or cupboard, to ensure maximum freshness. We also like to freeze freshly dried chiles to preserve their natural oils. Flash freeze them in a single layer on a sheet pan so they don't stick together, then transfer to an airtight freezer bag, where they can hang out for up to 1 year in the freezer.

Epazote: A leafy herb with black pepper notes used throughout Mexican cooking, especially in beans. On more than one occasion, we call for fresh epazote, which can be found at most Mexican grocers. While not as flavorful, dried epazote can be swapped into most recipes (just double the quantity!), perhaps with the exception of the Squash Blossom Quesadillas (page 197) and Requesón Tetelas (page 202).

Escabeche Juice: When a dish is looking for a little flavor nudge, juice it up with this burst of "boom boom flavor power." Fermín adds the liquid from Escabeche (page 256) to salsas, anything with avocado, and micheladas, and now you can, too.

Good Attitude: Real talk: The worst dishes we have ever prepared can be directly linked to mala onda, or bad vibes. Cook with love. Taste the love.

Hot Sauce: Favorites include Valentina and Búfalo, sure, but it's San Luis that Fermín uses the most at home.

Lard: Don't skimp on the lard, friends. You might occasionally buy a cheap olive oil—no judgment—but cheap lard hits different. We love Porter Road, which ships nationally.

Masa Harina: Masa harina (masa flour) is dehydrated fresh masa, or dough, made from nixtamalized corn. We use masa harina for tamales, homemade corn tortillas, and several other applications throughout this cookbook. We tested all of the recipes using Masienda's masa flours and we are partial to their rich corn flavor, but any masa flour will do the trick. It is worth noting that varying moisture levels and particle sizes among brands will subtly impact their respective hydration processes. Remember, you can always add more dry masa flour to your hydrated masa if it seems to be feeling too wet; conversely, you can add more liquid if it's feeling too dry.

Mexican Oregano: More lemony than its Greek counterpart. Find it at some Mexican grocers and online at Rancho Gordo.

Morton Coarse Kosher Salt: Fermín is all in on Morton coarse kosher salt, as are Jorge's in-laws. This is a major hot take we look forward to discussing on late-night talk shows one day, as many chefs have a well-documented affinity for Diamond Crystal kosher salt, and this break with tradition is nothing short of revolutionary. All hyperbole aside, most dishes throughout this cookbook call for salt to taste, in which cases you can use any kosher salt you'd like. For recipes that specify an exact measurement of salt, however, we call for Morton, which *PLEASE NOTE* is not an even swap for Diamond Crystal. Due to their different production methods, Morton coarse kosher salt is denser and 50 percent saltier by volume than Diamond Crystal.

To demonstrate: 1 tablespoon of Morton coarse kosher weighs about 14.75 grams compared to 1 tablespoon of Diamond Crystal kosher, which weighs 9.75 grams; you will want to convert accordingly to avoid oversalting (for simplicity's sake: ½ teaspoon of Morton is equal to about 1 teaspoon of Diamond Crystal). Many thanks to Samin Nosrat for this breakdown from her best-selling cookbook *Salt, Fat, Acid, Heat*.

Neutral Oil: Sunflower, avocado, and grapeseed are some of our go-to's.

Onions: Another controversial perspective poised for its fifteen minutes of internet virality: Fermín, a Mexico-born-and-raised chef, personally and professionally uses yellow onions in all cooked applications to add a mellow sweetness. (He uses white onions for raw garnishes on things like tortas and tacos.) "Look, yellow onions are very un-Mexican of me, but isn't that what this cookbook is all about?" he asks. "Recipes inspired by Mexican street food, written in English, full of delicious contradictions?" We, for our part, see it that way and we invite you to incorporate your own personality and preferences with confidence as you cook your way through this book. When onion types are not specified in a recipe, Fermín intends for it to be made with yellow onion, but feel free to use white if that's what you have on hand.

Quesillo: Also known as Oaxacan cheese or queso Oaxaca, quesillo is a low-moisture string cheese similar in flavor, texture, and meltability to mozzarella. Mexican-made quesillo is traditionally produced with whole milk or double cream that may or may not be pasteurized. Suffice it to say, it is incredibly delicious and an unfair advantage when competing against most U.S.-produced quesillo made with ultrapasteurized skim milk, which typically yields a flavorless, waxy, plasticky result when melted. This ingredient is worth the extra shipping time it might require to get the good stuff. We are fans of Quesillo Real de Oaxaca, available on Amazon, and Queso Campesino. When a recipe calls for quesillo, it should be pulled apart by hand into thin strings and measured in loosely packed cups.

Salsas: "Don't buy them. Just make them."
—Fermín

Tamal Hojas: We will call for one of two types of hojas (leaves) for wrapping and steaming tamales: corn husks and banana leaves. When sourcing corn husks (hojas de maíz), we prize whole, flat hojas. Because of their residual moisture after drying, corn husks can be highly perishable and susceptible to mold if packaged without preservatives, such as acetic acid. While we prefer untreated hojas, they can be tough to find commercially, and we understand why: No one wants a tamal wrapped in mold. So, if you are finding that your corn husks smell sharply of acid, plan to soak and rinse them a bit more than usual to render them neutral, or close to it. As for banana leaves (hojas de plátano), these are even more perishable than corn husks and are typically sold refrigerated or frozen. Banana leaves last up to a week refrigerated and six months when frozen.

Show, Don't Tell

While we appreciate cooking as a break from screen time, there are some techniques we feel are best expressed visually. So we've dropped QR codes into some of the recipes with harder-to-explain techniques. Give the code a scan with your smartphone for a quick video primer, then put the phone down and dive right back into the meditation of cooking. Scan the code above to view tutorials of all the cooking methods covered in the book, along with more videos to bring the recipes to life!

TOSTADAS

As far as cooking goes, does it really get any easier than toast?

Sure, when we get into toppings territory, difficulty levels can and will run the gamut, but it's hard to deny that toast is a pretty facile food at heart; and toast is where we're headed in this chapter . . . toast-adas, that is.

Tostadas are essentially crispy corn tortillas—the tortilla equivalent of toast. In fact, tostada literally means "toasted."

Of course, within this broad criterion, we get a fair number of variations on the theme. Tostadas can be deep-, shallow-, or air-fried, for instance; they can also be toasted on a comal or baked in an oven. Some corn tortillas are mixed with wheat flour or cooking starches to achieve extra bubbles when fried, while others, like Jalisco's famous raspadas, are scraped on one side while partially raw and then cooked through on a comal for an equally nuanced, craggy texture.

No matter the case, we see tostadas as an addictively simple entry point into the world of vitamina T, and hence, a fitting start to this cookbook.

Make no mistake, though: Just because tostadas are often served as an antojito (starter), they are not merely limited to appetizer status. Tinga Tostadas (page 51) are a regular dinner staple in most Mexican households, as are Asiento Tostadas (page 29), a Oaxacan snack, sure, but one that is exceedingly crushable and balanced enough to be consumed in entrée-sized quantities (especially for Jorge's kids).

Beyond the realm of street food where the tostadas have substantive toppings, they are also served as a textural foil to soups, stews, and dips, as well as being the tortilla format of choice for nearly all types of ceviche.

Within each of the following recipes, we have called for a specific type of tostada (e.g., baked, fried), but these are merely recommendations—approach as you see fit!

Si JEFA

Baked Tostadas

MAKES 4 TOSTADAS

- 4 corn tortillas, homemade (page 97) or store-bought
- 2 teaspoons olive oil (optional)
- Kosher salt (optional)

When it comes to homemade tostadas, many count on this method because it allows you to prepare larger batches at a time, as opposed to one or two tostadas at a time (like the comal and fry methods, respectively). If you are craving a bit more oomph, consider rubbing or brushing both sides of the tortillas with oil and giving them a light dusting of salt before baking. Feel free to fit as many tortillas as your sheet pan will hold without overlapping (our half-sheets comfortably hold six).

1. Preheat the oven to 350°F. Line a sheet pan with a wire rack.
2. If using olive oil and salt, brush both sides of each tortilla with the oil to lightly coat and then sprinkle with salt. Place the tortillas on the wire rack without overlapping. If you want them super flat, place another wire rack on top of the tortillas.
3. Bake the tortillas until crunchy, about 25 minutes. Remove and let cool.

Fried Tostadas

MAKES 4 TOSTADAS

- 1½ cups neutral oil
- 4 corn tortillas, homemade (page 97) or store-bought
- Kosher salt

Special Equipment

- Candy/deep-fry thermometer (optional)

Scientifically speaking—no bias, really—fried tostadas just taste better. Their fatty, carby, salty goodness lights up those pleasure receptors in our brains and leaves us wanting mucho más. As it happens, however, the cleanup and leftover fry oil have been known to deter many from tackling this project at home, but that's what moderation and/or your preferred store-bought fried tostada alternatives are for, no?

1. In a large, deep sauté pan, heat the oil until the temperature reaches 350°F when checked with a candy/deep-fry thermometer. (If you don't have a thermometer, dip the handle of a wooden spoon into the oil. If the oil bubbles around the handle, it's hot enough.) Line a plate with paper towels and keep near the stove.
2. Working with one tortilla at a time, carefully drop the tortilla into the hot oil. Using a slotted spoon or fish spatula, gently press the tortilla down to keep it submerged in the oil and prevent its edges from curling up too much. When the tortilla is golden brown and the oil stops bubbling, 2 to 3 minutes, remove the tortilla from the pan and place it on the paper towel–lined plate to drain. Season to taste with salt. Repeat with the remaining tortillas, allowing the oil to come back to temperature before adding the next tortilla.

Comal Tostadas

MAKES 4 TOSTADAS

4 corn tortillas, homemade (page 97) or store-bought

Cooking for one or two? Don't feel like dealing with leftover frying oil or sheet-pan cleanup? The comal method is your quick-ish hack for knocking out a handful of tostadas in no time. Key to this method is ensuring that your tostadas in development do not kiss the bottom of the pan for too long, as they may develop more char than desired. Placing a wire rack on top of the tostadas halfway through the cooking process can help to keep them flat, but part of the beauty of tostadas al comal is their snowflake-like differences. The unevenness creates little dips and dents to catch extra sauce or filling.

1. Preheat a comal, griddle, or large skillet over medium-low heat.
2. When the comal is warm, place the tortillas on it without overlapping (depending on the size of your comal, you may want to work in batches). Cook the tortillas on each side for 6 minutes and flip, cooking on the other side for an additional 6 minutes. Continue flipping and cooking until all the moisture has been released from the tortillas and the tostadas are crisp to the touch, about 25 minutes total.

Asiento Tostadas

This might indeed be a snack commonly found among fondas and tlayuda vendors throughout Oaxaca, but that's never stopped us from eating four to fourteen of these at a time and collectively calling them an entrée. Core to this tostada's crushability is its modest smear of asiento—rendered pork fat mixed with bits of crispy crackling—that flavor-upgrades the iceberg lettuce from tasteless topping to steakhouse-grade wedge salad status. If you're looking for just a tad bit more substance, consider adding a layer of Smoky Refried Beans (page 238) during assembly (as pictured).

MAKES 4 TOSTADAS

4 Comal Tostadas (above) or store-bought tostadas

¼ cup Asiento (page 255)

1 cup crumbled queso fresco

Shredded iceberg lettuce, for serving

Salsa de Molcajete (page 251), for serving

1. Preheat the oven to 350°F. (Alternatively, heat a comal over medium-low heat.)
2. Dividing evenly, spread each tostada with the asiento and top with the queso fresco. Place all the dressed tostadas on a sheet pan.
3. Bake for 5 minutes or until the asiento and cheese are slightly melted. (If using a comal, warm each tostada one at a time until the cheese begins to melt.)
4. To serve, top each tostada with shredded lettuce and salsa.

Esquites Tostadas

MAKES 4 TOSTADAS

- 4 Baked Tostadas (page 26), Comal Tostadas (page 29), or store-bought tostadas
- 2 cups Smoky Refried Beans (page 238, made with pinto beans)
- Lime mayonnaise (preferably McCormick or homemade, recipe follows)
- 4 cups Esquites (page 33)

Garnishes

- Crumbled queso fresco
- Cilantro leaves
- Tajín or Aleppo pepper
- Lime wedges

There is something especially delightful about this textural combination, like the sensory satisfaction of stepping on fresh bubble wrap. With each bite, you get the captivating crunch of the toasted tortilla coupled with intermittent bursts of juicy corn pops. Purists can skip the tostada and refried beans altogether and go straight for the esquites themselves. Pro tip: A little extra dab of Búfalo salsa clásica picante never hurts on this tostada.

Spread each tostada with a thin layer of beans, then add a thin layer of lime mayonnaise, followed by a generous scoop of esquites (really pile it on; it should be 1 cup per tostada). Sprinkle the tostadas with the queso fresco, cilantro, and Tajín, then give them each a squeeze of lime.

Lime Mayonnaise

You can make as much or as little lime mayonnaise as you want. Just mix 5 parts mayonnaise with 1 part lime juice.

MAKES 1½ CUPS

- 1¼ cups mayonnaise (such as Hellmann's)
- ¼ cup fresh lime juice (about 2 limes)

In a small bowl, combine the mayonnaise and lime juice and stir until well combined. The lime mayonnaise can be stored in an airtight container in the fridge for up to 7 days.

RECIPE CONTINUES →

Esquites

MAKES 5 CUPS IF USING CACAHUAZINTLE, OR 4 CUPS IF USING FRESH CORN

1¼ cups dried cacahuazintle corn, or 3 cups fresh white corn kernels (about 4 ears)

1 tablespoon cal (calcium hydroxide; if using dried cacahuazintle corn)

4 cups chicken stock (preferably low-sodium)

1 cup roughly chopped onion

¼ cup (packed) fresh epazote

1 serrano chile, stemmed and halved lengthwise

1 teaspoon Morton kosher salt

While fresh cacahuazintle, a large-kernel corn varietal, is traditionally used for esquites, sweet corn makes a delicious substitute here. Serve the esquites on tostadas or in cups topped with queso, crema, lime, and Tajín.

1. If using dried cacahuazintle corn, bring 4 cups of water to a boil over medium-high heat, then reduce the heat to medium-low and add the dried corn and cal. Cook at a simmer for 12 minutes and then remove from the heat. Allow the corn to soak in the water for 1 hour. Strain and rinse thoroughly.
2. In a large pot, combine the drained corn or the fresh corn, chicken stock, onion, epazote, serrano, and salt, and bring to a boil over medium-high heat. Reduce the heat to a simmer and cook until the corn becomes tender and the grains look swollen, about 3 hours for the dried corn or about 20 minutes for the fresh. Add more water as needed to keep the corn covered.
3. Discard the epazote and serrano and drain the corn.

Red Snapper Ceviche Tostadas

MAKES 4 TOSTADAS

- 1 pound skinless red snapper fillet
- ½ cup fresh lime juice (about 3 limes)
- 1 teaspoon Morton kosher salt, plus more as needed
- 1 cup finely diced ripe beefsteak tomato (about 1 medium)
- 1 serrano chile, stemmed and thinly sliced into rounds
- ½ jalapeño chile, stemmed and thinly sliced into rounds
- ¼ cup finely diced red onion (about ½ small)
- ¼ cup finely diced white onion (about ½ small)
- 2 tablespoons minced cilantro (leaves and tender stems)
- 4 Fried Tostadas (page 26) or store-bought tostadas
- Salsa Taquera (page 246) or hot sauce, for serving

Despite its utterly simple preparation, ceviche persistently manages to be one of those dishes more regularly ordered out than prepared at home. We get it—working with raw fish can seem intimidating to the beginner or amateur cook, but hear us out: If you can confidently make toast, you can competently make ceviche, y'all. Give this recipe a whirl, and if you aren't satisfied, your next meal is on Este restaurant.* Thanks, Fermín.

*Este's accounting and legal teams did not approve this message, but here's to trying!

1. Dice the snapper into ¼-inch pieces. It doesn't have to be perfect, but the smaller the pieces, the better the fish will cure in the lime juice.
2. In a nonreactive bowl, combine the diced snapper, the lime juice, and salt. Stir and allow to marinate until the fish begins to turn slightly opaque, 5 to 10 minutes.
3. Add the tomato, chiles, onion, and cilantro. Taste and season with salt as needed.
4. Top each tostada with the ceviche and serve with the salsa taquera or your favorite hot sauce.

Beef Salpicón Tostadas

MAKES 4 TOSTADAS

Beef Salpicón

- ½ cup finely diced Russet potato (about 1 small)
- 3 packed cups (1 pound) Pulled Brisket (page 80)
- ⅓ cup thawed frozen peas
- ⅓ cup finely diced carrot (about ½ medium)
- 1 jalapeño chile, stemmed and minced
- ¼ cup lime mayonnaise (preferably McCormick or homemade, page 30)
- Juice of 1 lime
- Kosher salt

Tostadas

- 2 cups shredded iceberg lettuce (about ¼ head)
- Juice of 1 lime
- Kosher salt
- 4 Comal Tostadas (page 29) or store-bought tostadas
- 1 avocado, sliced, for garnish
- 2 radishes, thinly sliced, for garnish
- Escabeche, homemade (page 256) or store-bought, for serving
- Salsa Tatemada (page 247), for serving

As our abuelitas would regularly remind us, "¡Hay comida en la casa!" ("There is food in the house!"), which meant it was time to repurpose last night's leftovers. And to many of us, nothing says leftovers like salpicón, a seemingly motley assortment of oft-improvised ingredients, from seafood to chicken to beef. Salpicón de res (beef) is a northern Mexican shredded beef salad of sorts—a salad not quite in a lettuce-y kind of way but, rather, in the way an egg salad or a Charleston chicken salad improbably manages to be called a "salad." And somehow it always manages to stick the landing.

1. **Make the beef salpicón:** In a small saucepan, combine the potato with enough water to cover by 1 inch. Bring to a boil over medium-high heat. Reduce to a simmer and cook until the potato is tender, 7 to 10 minutes. Drain and let cool for 5 minutes, then place in a large bowl.
2. Add the pulled brisket, peas, carrot, jalapeño, lime mayonnaise, and lime juice to the bowl. Mix until fully combined, season to taste with salt, and set aside.
3. **Assemble the tostadas:** In a small bowl, toss together the lettuce, lime juice, and a pinch of salt.
4. Divide the seasoned lettuce among the 4 tostadas and top each with about ½ cup of the salpicón. Garnish with the avocado and radish slices and serve with the escabeche and salsa on the side. Store any leftover salpicón in an airtight container in the fridge for 4 to 6 days.

Chicken Tostadas "a la Siberia"

MAKES 4 TOSTADAS

Chicken

- 1 pound boneless, skinless chicken breasts
- 3 celery stalks, trimmed and cut into thirds
- 1 large onion, quartered
- 1 head of garlic, halved horizontally
- 1 bay leaf
- 2 teaspoons Morton kosher salt

Tostadas

- ½ cup Guacamole (page 255)
- 8 Baked Tostadas (page 26) or store-bought tostadas
- Kosher salt
- ½ cup Mexican crema
- Escabeche, homemade (page 256) or store-bought, for serving

Special Equipment

- Instant-read digital thermometer (optional)

Shortly after relocating to Monterrey, Mexico, from Puebla in the 1940s, brothers Demetrio and Francisco Téllez opened a food truck-ternt-restaurant near the city's bus terminal that would earn them regiomontana fame for generations to come. As the Téllez family legend goes, Demetrio and Francisco—both self-described history buffs with a deep-cut love for Russia's prehistoric Siberian era—named this cold, cream-topped, vertically engineered dish (and the restaurant it eventually inspired) in honor of that region's epic snow-capped mountains. Better yet, the sandwich-style construction of the top and bottom tostadas cheekily called to mind the table etiquette of said prehistoric tribes who ate exclusively with their hands. That's some major Vitamina T Energy (VTE) right there.

1. **Prepare the chicken:** In a medium soup pot, combine the chicken, celery, onion, garlic, bay leaf, and salt. Add enough water to cover the ingredients and bring to a boil over medium-high heat. Reduce the heat and simmer until the chicken is fully cooked (165°F) or when the meat is white when cut into, making sure to skim off any foam that forms on the surface, 20 to 25 minutes.
2. Remove the chicken from the pot and place in a bowl to cool. (Reserve the chicken stock for future use. Strain into an airtight container and store in the fridge for 5 to 7 days or in the freezer for 2 to 3 months.)
3. When the chicken is cool enough to handle, use clean hands or 2 forks to shred it as finely as possible, repeating the shredding process if necessary to produce thin strands of chicken. The fine texture of the chicken is what makes this tostada so special.
4. **Assemble the tostadas:** Spread 2 tablespoons of the guacamole on top of a tostada, then top with a generous amount of shredded chicken. Season with salt and follow with a big dollop of the crema. Top with a second tostada to make a tostada "sandwich." Repeat to make 4 "sandwiches." Serve with the escabeche on the side.

Beet-Avocado Tostadas

MAKES 4 TOSTADAS

- 3 large red beets, greens removed
- 1½ teaspoons Morton kosher salt, plus more as needed
- ¼ cup neutral oil
- ¼ cup raw peanuts, preferably whole
- 2 garlic cloves, thinly sliced
- 2 dried puya (pulla) chiles, stemmed, seeded, veins removed, and chopped
- 4 morita chiles, stemmed, seeded, and chopped
- ¼ cup golden raisins
- 1 avocado, halved
- 3 tablespoons fresh lime juice (about 2 limes)
- 4 Fried Tostadas (page 26) or store-bought tostadas
- Habanero-Pickled Onions (page 257), for garnish

Special Equipment

- Candy/deep-fry thermometer

This dish was on Suerte's opening "Vitamina T" menu, and it counts as the only recipe from the restaurant to be immortalized in this cookbook because: (1) it's just that special, and (2) we couldn't stand waiting for the official Suerte cookbook any longer, Fermín. Here, boiled beets are tossed in a smoky-sweet-savory peanut-based salsa macha and rounded out with pickled red onions for an explosive finish.

1. In a medium pot, combine the beets and enough water to cover, then add enough salt until the water tastes like the sea. Cook over medium heat until the beets are tender, 45 minutes to 1 hour. Drain and let cool.
2. Meanwhile, in a small saucepan over low heat, warm the oil until the temperature reaches 200°F when checked with a candy/deep-fry thermometer, about 3 minutes. Add the peanuts and cook, stirring constantly with a wooden spoon, until they are golden brown, about 5 minutes.
3. Add the garlic and cook for 1 minute, stirring constantly so it doesn't burn, then turn off the heat. Stir in the puyas, moritas, and raisins, and allow the chile oil to cool.
4. Scoop the avocado flesh into a small bowl and mash with the lime juice and salt. Taste and season with more salt as needed. Set aside.
5. Once the beets are cool enough to handle, peel them and cut into bite-size pieces. In a medium bowl, combine the beets, cooled chile oil, and salt to taste.
6. To assemble, spread the mashed avocado on each tostada, top with a generous scoop of beets, and garnish with the habanero-pickled onions.

Beef Tartare Tostadas

MAKES 4 TOSTADAS

- 10 ounces beef tenderloin
- ½ cup Pico de Gallo (page 000)
- Juice of 2 lemons
- 1 tablespoon olive oil
- Kosher salt
- ¼ cup Chipotle Mayo (page 253)
- 4 Baked Tostadas (page 26) or store-bought tostadas
- Cilantro leaves, for garnish

You don't find much raw meat in Mexican gastronomy, and this recipe is here to change that. In a dish like carne apache, the meat is technically "cooked" in lime juice like a ceviche, whereas this recipe is a full-on tartare sans the egg yolk. (Actually, there's still egg yolk, if you count the chipotle mayo, but you know what we mean.) With the lemon, mayo, and pico de gallo, there is plenty of tang, heat, and crunch to balance the rawness of the beef, but you can always cut the beef into smaller cubes or grind it entirely, if texture should present an issue.

1. Using a sharp knife, dice the beef into ¼-inch pieces. (Putting the beef in the freezer for 15 to 20 minutes before cutting may make this process easier, but it's not strictly necessary.)
2. In a medium bowl, toss together the cubed beef, the pico de gallo, lemon juice, olive oil, and salt to taste.
3. To assemble, spread the chipotle mayo on each tostada, top generously with the beef tartare, and garnish with the cilantro.

Roasted Butternut Squash Tostadas with Queso Fresco and Pomegranate

MAKES 4 TOSTADAS

1 medium butternut squash, halved and seeded

Kosher salt

Olive oil

1 cup Smoky Refried Beans (page 238, made with black beans), warmed

4 Baked Tostadas (page 26) or store-bought tostadas

Garnishes

1 cup crumbled queso fresco

¼ cup salted roasted pumpkin seeds

1 cup pomegranate arils (about 4 ounces; from 1 pomegranate)

Behold, friends, the holy trinity that is the milpa: corn, beans, and squash—plus some tasty garnishes sprinkled in for your eating pleasure. The Mesoamerican word milpa refers to both a cornfield and the complementary cultivation of corn, beans, and squash (a.k.a. the "three sisters" of agriculture). Together, these staples represent a fully balanced diet capable of catalyzing an entire civilization, as well as an enduring approach to regenerative farming, so go on and taste this milpa.

1. Preheat the oven to 400°F.
2. Season the butternut squash with salt and drizzle with olive oil. Place on a sheet pan cut-side up and bake until the squash is tender, about 45 minutes.
3. Allow the squash to cool. Scoop the flesh of the squash into a large bowl, discarding the skin. Mash with a fork, adding salt and olive oil to taste.
4. To assemble, place ¼ cup of the refried black beans on each tostada, followed by a generous scoop of butternut squash. Top with the queso fresco, pumpkin seeds, and pomegranate arils.

Vitamina T(ip)

Store any leftover butternut squash in an airtight container in the fridge for 3 to 5 days. You can use it to make more tostadas, of course, but it also makes a great filling for tacos dorados (see page 132) or a substitute for sweet potatoes in the Sweet Potato Costra Tacos (page 125).

Nutrition Facts
12 servings per container
Calories
45
BENIHANA of TOKYO

Ayocote Bean Tostadas with Queso Asadero

MAKES 4 TOSTADAS

- 2 cups ayocote morado beans (Masienda and Rancho Gordo both sell them)
- 6 tablespoons olive oil, plus more as needed
- 1 medium onion, roughly chopped
- 2 morita chiles, stemmed and seeded
- 2 pasilla chiles, stemmed, seeded, and veins removed
- 1 small bunch of dried epazote (optional)
- 2 dried avocado leaves (optional)
- Kosher salt
- 1 pound asadero or Muenster cheese, cut into four ½-inch-thick slices
- 4 Fried Tostadas (page 26) or store-bought tostadas

Special Equipment

- Blender

This is a real "naughty" dish, as Fermín is fond of describing those recipes that walk a fine line between comfort and indulgence. Here, we get our first taste together of the beloved costra, or crust, achieved in this case by searing asadero cheese over high heat. Queso asadero is to Mexican cuisine as halloumi is to the Middle Eastern kitchen: a high-protein, low-moisture, salty grilling cheese. By slicing the asadero to a ½-inch, steak-size thickness, the cooked result is a crispy, golden-brown outside and a gooey, molten inside that is hard to resist among most mortal eaters. Grounding it all are meaty (but positively vegetarian) ayocote beans prepared two ways—whole and pureed—and our crunchy tostada that makes for a nostalgic, nacho-like finish. Feel free to sub Muenster for the asadero, if you can't find it at your local grocery store.

1. In a large bowl, combine the beans with water to cover by 2 to 3 inches and soak for 4 to 6 hours, or preferably overnight.
2. In a heavy-bottomed soup pot over medium heat, warm the olive oil. Add the onion and sweat until translucent, about 7 minutes.
3. Add the chiles and cook until they start to release their oils and become fragrant, about 5 minutes.
4. Drain the beans and add to the pot along with enough water to cover the beans by 1 inch. If using, add the epazote and avocado leaves. Bring the beans to a boil, then reduce to a light simmer and cover. Cook until the beans are tender, 1½ to 3½ hours, testing every 30 minutes after the first hour. (The cook time will vary depending on the age of the beans.)
5. When the beans are tender, season them with salt. Discard the epazote and avocado leaves (if used).
6. Measure out 1½ cups of beans along with the chiles and onions and transfer to a blender. Puree until smooth, then set aside and keep warm. Cover the remaining beans to keep them warm in their broth.
7. On a lightly oiled comal, griddle, or large skillet over high heat, sear one slice of cheese at a time, on one side only, cooking until the edges turn golden brown, 1½ to 2 minutes. Repeat with the remaining slices.
8. To assemble, spread the pureed beans on each tostada. Using a slotted spoon, top with enough whole beans to cover the entire tostada. Place the cheese slices, seared sides up, atop the beans.

Vitamina T(ip)

Store any leftover cooked beans in their broth in an airtight container in the fridge for 3 to 5 days, or in the freezer for up to 6 months. Consider them your meal prep for the week—perfect with rice or in salads.

Cauliflower Ceviche Tostadas

MAKES 4 TOSTADAS

- 4 Baked Tostadas (page 26) or store-bought tostadas
- 4 cups Cauliflower Ceviche (recipe follows)
- ½ avocado, sliced
- Salsa Macha (page 252), for serving

Variations of this faux-fish dish have become de moda, or fashionable, on the internet recently, and with good reason: It's really tasty and sneaky-vegan to boot. Extra points (and antioxidants) if you make the ceviche multicolored, but straight white cauliflower will make this a full-on ceviche deepfake.

Top each tostada with about 1 cup of the ceviche and add a few slices of avocado, then serve with a drizzle of the salsa macha.

Cauliflower Ceviche

Steaming the cauliflower to an al dente texture and immediately shocking it in an ice bath is mission-critical, or else you'll end up with a mushy mess of a ceviche. Remember, we will be "cooking" the cauliflower further with the lime juice, so don't wing it with the steam time on this one, ya' hear? If you aren't making this for a tostada topping, serve it on its own with chips.

MAKES 5½ CUPS

- 1 medium head of cauliflower, trimmed and cored
- 1 cup finely diced ripe Roma (plum) tomato (about 1 medium)
- ½ cup fresh lime juice (about 3 limes)
- 1 serrano chile, stemmed and thinly sliced into rounds
- 1 jalapeño chile, stemmed and thinly sliced into rounds
- ¼ cup finely diced red onion (about ½ small)
- ¼ cup finely diced white onion (about ½ small)
- 2 tablespoons minced cilantro
- Kosher salt

Special Equipment

- Steamer basket/insert

1. Fill a large bowl with ice cubes and water, and keep near the stove. In a pot that fits a steamer basket or insert, add two inches of water and bring to a boil. Place the cauliflower in a steamer basket or insert, set it over the boiling water, cover the pot, and steam the whole head of cauliflower for 6 minutes. Immediately transfer the cauliflower to the ice bath to cool. (This is crucial for the proper texture of the ceviche.)
2. Cut the cooled cauliflower into bite-size pieces—as though you are chopping fish for ceviche.
3. In a large bowl, stir together the chopped cauliflower, the tomato, lime juice, serrano and jalapeño chiles, red and white onions, and cilantro. Season to taste with salt. Store the cauliflower ceviche in an airtight container in the fridge for 2 to 3 days.

Heirloom Tomato Tostadas with Avocado Puree

MAKES 4 TOSTADAS

- 1 avocado, halved
- Olive oil
- Juice of 2 limes
- ¾ teaspoon ground cumin
- Kosher salt
- 1 large or 2 small ripe heirloom tomatoes
- Flaky salt, such as Maldon
- 4 Baked Tostadas (page 26) or store-bought tostadas
- 1 serrano chile, stemmed and thinly sliced into rounds, for garnish
- 2 scallions (white and light green parts), thinly sliced, for garnish

Special Equipment

- Immersion blender

Sometimes, the most important ingredients are the ones you choose to leave out. This dish is a testament to that principle. Peak-season tomatoes, velvety avocados, crisp tostadas: You really don't need much else. Some might be inclined to call this a Mexican riff on bruschetta, but seeing as how tomatoes originated in Mexico, isn't it time to reclaim Italy's most popular antipasto in the name of tostadas, once and for all? Don't toss the leftover juice from the marinated tomatoes—it makes a delicious sangrita (tequila chaser).

1. Scoop the avocado flesh into a medium bowl or jar. Add 1 tablespoon of olive oil, half the lime juice, and the cumin. Using an immersion blender, puree until smooth. Season to taste with kosher salt.
2. Cut the tomatoes into irregular bite-size pieces. Season with olive oil, the remaining lime juice, and flaky salt.
3. Spread about ¼ cup of the avocado puree evenly on each tostada. Top each with the seasoned tomatoes and garnish with the serrano and scallions.

Sikil Pak Tostadas with Jicama and Purslane

MAKES 4 TOSTADAS

- 1 cup fresh purslane or watercress
- ½ cup finely diced peeled jicama
- Grated zest and juice of 1 lemon
- Kosher salt
- Olive oil
- 4 Comal Tostadas (page 29) or store-bought tostadas
- 1 cup Sikil Pak (recipe follows)

This plant-based tostada packs a powerful punch of healing powers, if you ask us. Sikil pak is a hearty Mayan salsa made of pepitas, or pumpkin seeds, with a texture akin to hummus. In addition to being luscious and delicious, the seeds themselves are chock-full of antioxidants, minerals, and healthy fats, and they have been linked to improved heart health, sleep quality, and even fertility. Topping things off are crunchy jicama and verdolagas (a.k.a. purslane), an edible succulent with a lemony flavor profile, deep ties to ancient Mesoamerican civilizations, off-the-charts omega-3 fatty acids, and ancestral culinary traditions that predate its cheffy use as a garnish by a couple thousand years, give or take. If you can't find purslane at your local farmers market or Mexican grocer, top with any herb(s) of your choice.

1. Pick the leaves from the purslane and reserve, discarding the stems. Chop the leaves into bite-size pieces and place in a small bowl. Add the jicama, lemon zest and juice, and the salt and olive oil to taste.
2. Spread each tostada evenly with the sikil pak and top with a sprinkling of the purslane salad.

Sikil Pak

Use sikil pak for tostadas or serve as a dip with tortilla chips.

MAKES 2½ CUPS

- 1 cup raw pumpkin seeds
- 4 large ripe Roma (plum) tomatoes
- 1 small onion, quartered
- 1 fresh habanero chile, seeded, depending on heat tolerance
- 2 tablespoons fresh orange juice (about ½ orange)
- 2 tablespoons fresh lime juice (about 1 lime)
- 3 tablespoons olive oil
- 1½ teaspoons Morton kosher salt, plus more as needed

Special Equipment

- Food processor or blender

1. On a dry comal, griddle, or large skillet over medium heat, toast the pumpkin seeds, stirring constantly to avoid burning them, until they start to smell fragrant and turn golden brown, 2 to 4 minutes. Transfer to a small bowl and set aside.
2. Increase the heat to medium-high and on the same comal, char the tomatoes, onion, and habanero, turning to blacken on all sides. Remove each vegetable once it is fully charred, 20 to 25 minutes total. (Since the habaneros are the smallest, they will be done the soonest, followed by the onion, and finally the tomatoes.) Remove the stem from the habanero when it is cool enough to handle.
3. In a food processor (or a blender, if you like a smoother puree), combine the tomatoes, onion, habanero, and pumpkin seeds, and pulse or blend until smooth. With the machine running, stream in the orange juice, lime juice, and then the olive oil, and blend until smooth. Add the salt and season to taste with more as needed. Store the sikil pak in an airtight container in the fridge for 5 to 7 days.

Tinga Tostadas

MAKES 4 TOSTADAS

Chicken Tinga

- Kosher salt
- 4 to 5 chipotle chiles in adobo sauce
- 4 dried puya (pulla) chiles, stemmed, seeded, and veins removed
- 4 ripe medium Roma (plum) tomatoes
- 1 pound boneless, skinless chicken breasts
- 1 bay leaf
- 4 garlic cloves, peeled
- 1 small onion, thinly sliced
- Neutral oil

Tostadas

- 4 Fried Tostadas (page 26) or store-bought tostadas
- Shredded iceberg lettuce, for garnish
- Crumbled queso fresco, for garnish

Special Equipment

Blender; instant-read digital thermometer (optional)

Tinga comes from the Nahuatl word tingatl, which means "to tear." As its ancestral name suggests, this dish is composed of torn or shredded meat—commonly chicken, though pork is believed to be the truest of the tinga OGs. Tinga has a reputation for being exceedingly easy to prepare and delicious to consume, but we felt compelled to give this tinga a lil' glow-up 'cause it's special like that . . . hence the blanched and peeled tomatoes and dried chiles.

1. Fill a 6-quart soup pot with about 4 quarts of water and salt the water as aggressively as you would for pasta water, then bring to a boil over medium-high heat.
2. Fill a bowl with ice cubes and water, and keep near the stove.
3. Meanwhile, in a medium bowl, combine the chipotle and puya chiles and enough hot water to cover. Soak the chiles until softened.
4. Use a paring knife to cut a small, shallow X on the bottom of each tomato (the opposite end to the stem end). Add the tomatoes to the boiling water and cook for 30 to 45 seconds, or until the skin around the X begins to loosen. With the water still boiling, remove the tomatoes and place in the ice bath until cool to the touch.
5. While the tomatoes cool, add the chicken and bay leaf to the pot. Reduce the heat to medium and simmer until the chicken is fully cooked (165°F) or when the meat is white when cut into, 20 to 25 minutes.
6. While the chicken is cooking, peel the tomatoes and place them in a blender. Drain the chiles from the hot water and add them to the blender along with the garlic and half of the onion, and blend until smooth.
7. Remove the chicken from the pot and place in a bowl to cool. (Reserve the chicken cooking liquid for future use. Strain into an airtight container and store in the fridge for 5 to 7 days or in the freezer for 2 to 3 months.) When the chicken is cool enough to handle, use clean hands or 2 forks to shred it as finely as possible.
8. Heat a medium skillet over medium heat and add just enough oil to coat the bottom (about 1 tablespoon). Cook the remaining onion until translucent, 2 to 3 minutes, then add the chicken and stir to combine.
9. Increase the heat to high and move the onion and chicken mixture to the sides of the pan, creating an empty space in the middle about 4 inches in diameter. Pour the pureed tomato mixture into that space; it will start to bubble and sizzle aggressively. Stir to incorporate the chicken into the sauce, and turn the heat back down to medium. Cook for 10 minutes, allowing the liquid to reduce. Taste and season with salt as needed.
10. Pile each tostada with the tinga and garnish with the shredded lettuce and crumbled cheese.

Vitamina T(ip)

If you have leftover tinga, serve it atop rice, or use it to fill enchiladas or flautas.

TORTAS

A product of cross-pollination between local and global ingredients

Some time roughly between the Spanish introduction of wheat to Mexico in the early 1500s and the gonzo culinary movement that is TikTok, the towering torta was born. A torta is Mexico's wide-ranging interpolation of the modern sándwich (that's Spanish, of course, for sandwich). Architecturally speaking, you take a roll such as a bolillo or telera—the foundational bread component—and add approximately one to one thousand layers of fillings, from cold cuts to chilaquiles (you read correctly; see page 66) and/or everything in between, and with some condiment cantilevers thrown in for good measure: ¡Jenga!, you have yourself a composed, if not structurally sound, torta.

As is often the case with most unbranded food innovations like the torta, taco, tamal, or tlacoyo, no one knows for certain just when that first baroque-influenced bolillo sammie was born, but modern-day leyendas seem to get us pretty close. Many point to Armando Martínez Centurión, who, they believe, opened the very first tortería, or torta shop, in Mexico City in 1892.

In many ways, the invention of the torta was as much a product of cross-pollination between local and global ingredients like beans (Mexico) and pork (Spain) as it was a polarizing expression of then-president Porfirio Díaz's politics of the day. It was, after all, during this period when his disciples unsuccessfully attempted to ban the corn tortilla in favor of white wheat bread, the European staple and preferred Porfirian symbol of Mexico's push toward modernity.

Despite their complex role in Mexican history, tortas have become as significant to vitamina T as any of their masa-based peers; and they just might be its foremost spectacle. Sure, this has always been an everyman kind of food of modest means, first designed with Mexico City's students and working class in mind, but that hasn't stopped its torteros from dabbling in over-the-top flourishes of showmanship and excess that would make Guy Fieri blush.

WC
LIMPIOS AL INTERIOR
DE LA PLAZA

Bolillos

MAKES 6 ROLLS

- 1 tablespoon active dry yeast
- 1½ cups (360g) warm (but not hot) water
- 4 cups (500g) all-purpose flour, plus more for dusting
- 1 tablespoon sugar
- 1 tablespoon Morton kosher salt
- 1 tablespoon unsalted butter or shortening, at room temperature
- Neutral oil

Special Equipment

- Stand mixer

How to Shape Bolillos

For all but a handful of occasions, tortas are assembled on either a telera or a bolillo. Teleras are oblong ciabatta-like rolls with two lengthwise indentations running along the top, while bolillos, our personal favorite, are somewhere between a squat, bánh mi–style baguette and a hoagie roll. You don't need to make your own bolillos to re-create the torta experience at home—go nuts with whatever bread thing brings you the most pleasure, from a traditional baguette to a brioche bun, Portuguese to kaiser roll—but this recipe is as straightforward and as simple as baking gets. If you're still dying to make a true telera, be sure to check out Roberto Santibañez's book, *Tacos, Tortas, and Tamales,* for his timeless take.

1. In a small bowl, stir the yeast into the warm water and let stand until bubbles form, about 10 minutes.
2. In a stand mixer fitted with the dough hook attachment, combine the yeast-water mixture with the flour and mix on low speed (setting 2 on a KitchenAid) until combined.
3. Add the sugar, salt, and butter, and mix on medium speed (setting 5 or 6) until the dough is smooth and springs back to the touch, 8 to 9 minutes.
4. Transfer the dough to a floured surface and shape into a ball. Place in a lightly oiled bowl and turn to coat with the oil. Cover the bowl with a clean kitchen towel and let the dough rise until doubled in size, anywhere from 30 to 60 minutes depending on the room temperature.
5. Turn out the dough onto a lightly floured surface and divide into 6 equal portions, rolling each portion into a ball.
6. Starting with the first ball you shaped, put your hands on each side of the dough. With your hands cupped, roll the dough into a football shape whose size should extend from your wrist to the tip of your middle finger. Repeat with the remaining dough balls. Need a visual cue? Scan the QR code.
7. Transfer the shaped bolillos to a sheet pan and cover with a clean kitchen towel to rise until the dough has nearly doubled in size, about 1 hour. The dough is ready to bake when it springs back two-thirds of the way when poked with a finger.
8. While the dough is rising, preheat the oven to 375°F.
9. When you are ready to bake, lightly dust a work surface with flour, and using a sharp knife or a razor blade, make a ¼-inch deep cut lengthwise down the top of each bolillo. Transfer the bolillos to a sheet pan.
10. Bake the bolillos for 8 to 16 minutes, until they are a deep golden brown, rotating the sheet pan front to back at the halfway mark. (Do not open the oven until 8 minutes have passed.)
11. Place the bolillos on a wire rack to cool, about 15 minutes. Store the bolillos individually wrapped in plastic at room temperature for 2 to 3 days.

FERMÍN'S TORTA TIPS

Mayo

McCormick Mayonesa con Jugo de Limones is to my favorite tortas as Duke's is to fried bologna sandwiches. Give it a whirl. If you can't find it, make your own Lime Mayonnaise (page 30).

Mustard

French's yellow mustard is my personal favorite, with a reliable acidity to cut all that delicious sodium.

Ham

This is where I will go against my cheffy instincts in favor of the most processed, traditionally Mexican cold cut that the fewest of pesos can buy: FUD (pronounced FOOD).

Queso

Another Spanish influence here. Most white cheese I see on tortas in Mexico is always called "Manchego," but this is for sure nothing like real Manchego. I personally recommend "quesadilla cheese," not to be confused with the ubiquitous shredded "Mexican-style" cheese blends.

Heat

I like adding heat by way of chipotles in adobo, my preferred ones being from La Morena, of course.

More sodium

I know many of these tortas are high in salt content already, but a flaky sea salt like Maldon is clutch for bringing those tomatoes and avocados into full relief.

Pickled stuff

I don't like to toot my own horn, but I'm really damn proud of my Escabeche (page 256), so beep beep. If I'm not making it from scratch, canned escabeche from La Morena, Herdez, or La Costeña will still get the job done.

Bun scrape

Some of these tortas are absolutely enormous and can be difficult to eat without scraping out some of the bun's interior. This is not only necessary for an optimal eating experience but encouraged.

Fermín's Escabeche (see page 256)

McCORMICK
SLICED
PICKLED
grateful

Chicken Milanesa Torta

MAKES 2 TORTAS

- 2 boneless, skinless chicken breasts (about 8 ounces each)
- ½ tablespoon Morton kosher salt, plus more as needed
- ¼ teaspoon freshly ground black pepper
- ½ cup all-purpose flour
- 2 large eggs, beaten
- ½ cup fine dried bread crumbs (such as Progresso)
- Neutral oil
- 2 bolillos, homemade (page 57) or store-bought
- ¼ cup Smoky Refried Beans (page 238, made with black beans), warmed
- 1 cup shredded iceberg lettuce
- ¼ cup lime mayonnaise (preferably McCormick or homemade, page 30)
- ½ avocado, halved
- 1 small ripe tomato, cut into ½-inch-thick slices
- Escabeche, homemade (page 256) or store-bought, for serving

***Eat mor' chikin'. Finger-lickin' good. Have it your way.* Don't mind if we do. This fried chicken torta sees these fast-food sandwich legends and raises them with an unstoppable combination of refried beans, avocado, mayo, AND crema, not to mention all that crunchy shrettuce, baby. Dear God, grant us the serenity to accept the things we cannot change, the courage to change the crispy chicken sandwiches that we can, and the restraint to not eat at least one of these tortas for breakfast, lunch, and dinner for the rest of our time on Earth. Amen.**

1. Pound the chicken breasts to a ¼-inch thickness.
2. Set up a dredging station in 3 shallow bowls. In one bowl, mix the flour with the ½ tablespoon salt and the ¼ teaspoon pepper. Place the beaten eggs in a second bowl. Spread the bread crumbs in a third. To bread the chicken, lightly dust each piece with the seasoned flour, then dip in the beaten egg, then coat with the bread crumbs.
3. Pour enough oil into a wide, shallow frying pan so that it will come halfway up the sides of the chicken when added. Warm the oil over medium heat. Line a plate with paper towels and keep near the stove.
4. When the oil is hot, pan-fry the chicken until golden brown on both sides, 3 to 4 minutes. Depending on the size of your pan, you might have to do this one piece at a time. When cooked, transfer the chicken to the paper towels to drain.
5. Slice the bolillos in half lengthwise. Heat a comal, griddle, or large skillet over medium-high heat. Toast the bolillos cut-side down until golden. This will add a layer of texture to prevent the torta from getting too soggy.
6. On the bottom half of each bolillo, thinly spread about 2 tablespoons of the refried black beans, then place a piece of chicken on top of each. Add the shredded lettuce.
7. On the top half of each bolillo, spread the lime mayonnaise. Add the avocado and lightly smash it with a fork, allowing the mayo and avocado to blend. Top with the tomato and season with salt, then sandwich the buns together.
8. Serve immediately, with escabeche on the side.

TORTAS GIGANTES
HUARACHES
AGUAS Y LICUADOS
TORTAS
GIGANTES

Guacamaya

MAKES 2 TORTAS

- 2 bolillos, homemade (page 57) or store-bought
- 2 tablespoons lime mayonnaise (preferably McCormick or homemade, page 30)
- ½ avocado, sliced
- 2 ounces chicharrones (preferably from a Mexican butcher shop)
- ½ cup cueritos (pickled pork rinds; optional)
- Pico de Gallo (page 253), for garnish
- Salsa de Chile de Árbol (page 250), for serving

Guacamaya, Spanish for macaw, supposedly earns its name from the squawking, whistling, screeching, bird-like range of sounds that could be heard by the first person (in León, Mexico) to ever eat this spicy torta. Rest assured, this version is only mildly hot, not Da-Bomb-Beyond-Insanity hot (until you add that salsa de chile de árbol), and is actually more of a study in textures than in capsaicin.

Slice the bolillos in half lengthwise, making sure to not cut all the way through (they should look like hot dog buns, rather than separated halves). Lightly spread the mayo on both halves of each bolillo. Dividing evenly, fill each roll with the avocado, chicharrones, and cueritos (if using). Garnish with a generous amount of pico de gallo and serve with the salsa de chile de árbol on the side.

VITAMINA C(HICHARRÓN)

If you've ever been to a Mexican butcher, you'll well know that a chicharrón is a shape-shifting delicacy that can and will assume multiple forms. Here now, then, is the one and only key you'll ever need to select your chicharrones in the wild.

1 Chicharrón

An airy, puffy, fried pork skin—simple as that. This is the only type we use in this cookbook.

2 Chicharrón de harina

No, you won't find this at a butcher, and that's because it's made of wheat flour, not pork. It can be a dead ringer for the real stuff, so stay alert out there. That said, it's still very delicious with Valentina and lime.

3 Chicharrón prensado clásico

Imagine Surtido Carnitas (page 109) in adobo with an occasional dash of pink salt pressed together until it binds into a tight-looking terrine shape. This winds up in vitamina T classics like tlacoyos, sopes, and gorditas and is particularly addictive in texture (think bacon bits) and flavor (chorizo), if you ask us.

4 Chicharrón prensado (natural)

Same concept as chicharrón prensado clásico, but without the adobo (and dye that can sometimes accompany it) that otherwise gives it a bright red chorizo color. Shown here in its crumbled state.

5 Chicharrón carnudo

This basically translates to "fleshy pork rind." It's a little bit of puffy skin and a little bit of chewy meat, all in one bite.

1
2
3
4
5

Guajolota

MAKES 2 TORTAS

- 2 bolillos, homemade (page 57) or store-bought
- ¼ cup lime mayonnaise (preferably McCormick or homemade, page 30)
- 2 tamales (such as Chicken in Mole Verde Tamales, page 162)
- ½ cup Salsa Verde (page 245)
- ¼ cup grated Cotija cheese
- ¼ cup Mexican crema

Arguably the greatest carb-on-carb combo since rice and beans, pizza and potatoes, or tamales and atole (see page 174), guajolotas are tamal-filled tortas. Before the deniers claim this is not a thing, please trust that it most definitely is—from CDMX, no less, and with roots that date as far back as nearly two centuries. Bearing the Spanish name for a female turkey, they are controversial in their excess, maximalist in their design, and—just in case you were wondering—they couldn't care less what you, we, or anyone else has to say about them.

1. Slice the bolillos in half lengthwise, making sure to not cut all the way through (they should look like hot dog buns, rather than separated halves). Spread the mayonnaise on both sides of each bolillo.
2. Heat a comal, griddle, or large skillet over medium-high heat. Toast the bolillos cut-side down until golden. This will add a layer of texture to prevent the torta from getting too soggy.
3. Warm the tamales using the method of your choice (see "Tamales Like It Hot," page 152).
4. Place a tamal inside each bolillo and cover the tamales evenly with the salsa verde, Cotija, and crema.

Chilaquiles Torta

Depending on how fast you eat this torta and the salsa-smothered totopos that constitute its filling, each bite can go in one of two directions: soft and crispy or soft and soft(er). You might order one torta de chilaquiles fresh and eat it promptly without missing a beat, for instance; or you might shuffle back into bed, assume the fetal position with a trash bin close by, and eat that same torta twelve hours later at room temperature, along with an ice-cold Electrolit. No matter the scenario, both directions have a special place in our hungover hearts.

MAKES 2 TORTAS

- 2 bolillos, homemade (page 57) or store-bought
- ¼ cup Smoky Refried Beans (page 238, made with black beans), warmed
- Chilaquiles Verdes (page 222), without egg or garnishes, warmed

Garnishes

- ¼ medium red onion, thinly sliced
- ¼ cup Mexican crema
- ½ cup grated Cotija cheese
- Cilantro leaves

1. Slice the bolillos in half lengthwise, making sure to not cut all the way through (they should look like hot dog buns, rather than separated halves).
2. Heat a comal, griddle, or large skillet over medium-high heat. Toast both sides of each bolillo until golden. This will add a layer of texture to prevent the torta from getting too soggy.
3. Spread the refried black beans on the bottom half of each bolillo. Top each bolillo bottom with the chilaquiles and garnish with the onion, crema, cheese, and cilantro. Close the tortas with the bolillo tops and enjoy.

Ham and Egg Torta

MAKES 2 TORTAS

- 2 bolillos, homemade (page 57) or store-bought
- Neutral oil
- 2 ounces thinly sliced deli ham, cut into 1-inch squares
- 5 large eggs
- Kosher salt and freshly ground black pepper
- ½ cup Smoky Refried Beans (page 238, made with black beans), warmed
- ½ avocado, sliced
- Pico de Gallo (page 253), for garnish

This is the closest thing to breakfast tacos, a staple of Fermín's adopted hometown, that you can find in northern Mexico. Unlike breakfast tacos, though, these tortas can easily be assembled now and eaten later, without the whole thing falling apart on you.

1. Slice the bolillos in half lengthwise, cutting all the way through. Heat a lightly oiled comal, griddle, or large skillet over medium-high heat. Toast the bolillos on both sides until golden. This will add a layer of texture to prevent the tortas from getting too soggy. Set aside.

2. Heat a large nonstick skillet over medium heat and warm a bit of oil. Fry the ham until it starts to get a bit of color and the edges begin to crisp, 1 to 2 minutes. Crack in the eggs, season with salt and pepper, and scramble until the eggs are fully cooked but not dry.

3. To assemble the tortas, lightly spread the refried black beans on the bottom half of each bolillo. Pile the scrambled eggs atop the beans, then top with the avocado and pico de gallo. Close the tortas with the bolillo tops.

Chorizo and Potato Pambazo

MAKES 2 TORTAS

- 4 guajillo chiles, stemmed, seeded, and veins removed
- Kosher salt
- 1 russet potato, peeled and medium diced, placed in cold water to prevent browning
- 1 cup uncooked Chorizo Rojo (page 237)
- 2 bolillos, homemade (page 57) or store-bought
- Neutral oil

Garnishes

- Shredded iceberg lettuce
- Mexican crema
- Crumbled Cotija cheese

Special Equipment

- Blender

Looking at this torta, it's hard not to think of "Lunch Lady Land" in the very best of ways. Anyone? Well, to us, the pambazo may just be the inspiration for the [*hot take*] inferior Sloppy Joe, where ground mystery meat is replaced with only the very finest fluorescent chorizo rojo. Don't for a second think you can skip the crucial step of soaking the bolillo in guajillo puree—it makes the torta.

1. In a small bowl, combine the chiles and enough hot water to cover. Soak the chiles until softened, about 15 minutes.
2. Transfer the chiles along with some of their soaking liquid to a blender and puree until smooth, adding additional soaking water as needed to create a smooth, thin salsa. Season to taste with salt and pour into a bowl large enough to fit the bolillos. Set aside.
3. In a medium saucepan, combine the potato with salted water to cover. Bring to a boil over medium-high heat. Reduce to a simmer and cook the potato until tender, 5 to 7 minutes. Drain the potato.
4. In a medium sauté pan over medium-low heat, cook the chorizo, breaking it up with a wooden spoon, until it begins to release its juices and is no longer pink, about 5 minutes. Add the potato and stir to combine. When the chorizo is fully cooked and browned, about 5 minutes more, season to taste with salt and remove from the heat.
5. Add the uncut bolillos to the bowl with the guajillo salsa and toss until coated in liquid.
6. Heat a lightly oiled comal, griddle, or large skillet over medium-high heat. Toast the soaked bolillos on both sides. This will add a layer of texture to slightly caramelize the salsa and prevent the torta from getting too soggy.
7. To assemble the tortas, slice the bolillos in half lengthwise. Spread the chorizo-potato mixture on the bottom half of each bolillo and garnish with the shredded lettuce, crema, and cheese, then cover with the top half of the bun.

Pork Adobada "del Beis" Torta

MAKES 2 TORTAS

- 8 guajillo chiles, stemmed, seeded, and veins removed
- 2 cascabel chiles, stemmed and seeded
- ¼ cup neutral oil, plus more for the grill
- 3 garlic cloves, peeled
- ½ cup cilantro (leaves and tender stems)
- ⅓ cup roughly chopped red onion (about ¼ onion)
- 3½ teaspoons Chipotle Puree (recipe follows)
- Kosher salt
- 10 ounces boneless pork loin, cut into ¼-inch-thick slices
- 2 bolillos, homemade (page 57) or store-bought
- ¼ cup lime mayonnaise (preferably McCormick or homemade, page 30)
- ½ avocado, sliced
- 1 medium ripe tomato, sliced
- ¼ medium white onion, thinly sliced
- 1 serrano chile, stemmed and thinly sliced

Special Equipment

Blender; charcoal or gas grill; instant-read digital thermometer (optional)

Fermín, here. This one is a special torta, or as we call them back home, lonche. My childhood home in Torreón was right across the street from a gas station that housed a local torta institution called Lonches de Adobada del Beis. The "del Beis" (pronounced BASS, as in "boom, badoom, boom, boom, badoom, boom, *bass*") was a reference to its origins as a popular baseball (béisbol) stadium food. While this would make one absurdly huge torta, here we split the fillings across two bolillos in case you want to share or can't unhinge your jaw completely.

1. In a large bowl, combine the guajillo and cascabel chiles and enough hot water to cover. Soak the chiles until soft, about 10 minutes.
2. Meanwhile, in a medium sauté pan over medium-high heat, warm the oil. Add the garlic and cook, stirring occasionally, until soft and golden brown all over, about 8 minutes.
3. Drain the chiles, reserving some of their soaking liquid. In a blender, combine the chiles, the fried garlic and its cooking oil, the cilantro, red onion, and chipotle puree, and blend until it forms a smooth, thick adobo paste. Add a bit of the reserved chile-soaking liquid as needed to keep the blender moving. Season to taste with salt.
4. Add the pork to a medium bowl and lightly salt it all over. Rub the pork with the adobo paste, cover, and marinate in the fridge for 25 minutes or up to overnight.
5. When you are ready to cook the pork, prepare a charcoal or gas grill for high heat. Clean and oil the grates. Grill the pork over the hottest part of the grill until fully cooked (145°F), or until the exterior is charred and the adobo paste darkens in color, 2 to 3 minutes per side.
6. To assemble the tortas, split the bolillos lengthwise. Spread the mayo on the top halves. On the bottom half of each, add the avocado and smash with a fork, spreading the avocado over the bun, then season with salt. Dividing evenly, top the avocado with the grilled pork, tomato, white onion, and serrano. Close the tortas with the bolillo tops and enjoy.

Chipotle Puree

This simple condiment makes a great add-in or base for mayos, marinades, or salsas. It will keep in an airtight container in the fridge for 3 to 4 weeks (and virtually forever in the freezer).

In a small blender or mini food processor, process the chiles with the adobo sauce until you get a smooth puree.

MAKES ABOUT ¾ CUP

- 1 (7-ounce) can chipotle chiles in adobo (La Morena is our pick)

Special Equipment

Blender or mini food processor

Cubana Torta

MAKES 2 TORTAS

- Neutral oil
- 1 cup Surtido Carnitas (page 109)
- 2 salchichas rojas (Mexican red sausages), split in half lengthwise
- 4 slices Mexican Manchego cheese or Muenster
- 2 bolillos, homemade (page 57) or store-bought
- ¼ cup lime mayonnaise (preferably McCormick or homemade, page 30)
- 1 avocado, halved and sliced
- Flaky sea salt, such as Maldon
- ¼ cup yellow mustard
- ¼ cup Smoky Refried Beans (page 238, made with black beans)
- 4 thick-cut slices deli ham (about 5 ounces)
- 2 Steak Milanesas (page 76)
- 1 medium ripe tomato, sliced
- ½ medium white onion, thinly sliced
- Escabeche, homemade (page 256) or store-bought, for serving

As a Versailles-and-La Carreta–blooded Miami native, I (Jorge) can unequivocally tell you that this torta has nothing to do with the cubano, or Cuban sandwich, which is composed of lechón (roast pork that is invariably drier than it should be), ham, Swiss cheese, pickles, and yellow mustard. I can also tell you—in confidence, of course—that the torta cubana is better, at least for me personally *because condiments*. Truth be told, I've always preferred a medianoche to a cubano, but that's a whole different matter entirely. Legend has it that this creation took its name from a spot that used to sling tortas on República de Cuba in Mexico City in the 1950s.

1. On a lightly oiled comal, griddle, or large skillet over medium heat, sear the carnitas and the split sausages over medium heat to achieve a little bit of caramelization. When the sausages have developed some color, about 6 minutes, flip them over. Place the cheese slices on top of the sausages, allow the cheese to melt, then remove from the heat and set aside.
2. To assemble the tortas, split the bolillos in half lengthwise. Heat a comal, griddle, or large skillet over medium-high heat. Toast both sides of each bolillo until golden. This will add a layer of texture to prevent the torta from getting too soggy.
3. Spread the mayo on the top halves of the bolillos, then add the avocado. Smash the avocado with a fork, allowing the mayo and avocado to blend. Sprinkle with flaky sea salt.
4. Generously spread the mustard on the bottom halves of the bolillos to cover edge to edge, followed by a thin layer of refried beans. Place the carnitas on top, then the ham slices, followed by the sausage with cheese, and a steak milanesa on each. Top with the tomato and more flaky sea salt, then add the onions. Close the tortas with the bolillo tops and serve with the escabeche on the side.

Butternut Squash in Chile Colorado Torta

MAKES 2 TORTAS

- ½ cup olive oil
- 4 garlic cloves, peeled
- 6 pasilla chiles, stemmed, seeded, and veins removed
- 1 tablespoon cumin seeds, toasted and ground
- 1 small butternut squash, peeled and roughly diced
- 1 cup roughly diced peeled russet potato (about 1 large)
- Kosher salt
- 2 bolillos, homemade (page 57) or store-bought
- ¼ cup lime mayonnaise (preferably McCormick or homemade, page 30)
- ½ avocado, sliced
- 2 cups (loosely packed) hand-pulled strands quesillo (a.k.a. queso Oaxaca), or 1½ cups shredded low-moisture mozzarella
- ¼ medium white onion, thinly sliced

Special Equipment

- Blender

You won't find this torta on any tortería menus in Mexico, because Fermín developed it just for you, friends. This recipe takes its inspiration from chile colorado, a chile-infused braise of either beef or pork, but it goes full-on vegetarian here with a butternut-squash-and-potato base. While you might still be tempted to go classic carnivore on this number, remember that a good quesillo cheese is chock-full of delicious protein and salt, which gives this torta the meaty quality that brings it all together.

1. In a medium saucepan over medium heat, warm the oil. Add the garlic and fry until golden brown, 6 to 7 minutes. Remove the garlic and set aside.
2. In the same saucepan over medium heat, cook the chiles, stirring constantly to prevent them from burning. When chiles begin to toast and become fragrant, remove them from the pan and set aside to cool.
3. Set the same saucepan with the now-infused olive oil over medium heat. Add the cumin, followed immediately by the butternut squash and potato. Reduce the heat to medium-low and cover.
4. In a blender, combine the cooled chiles, fried garlic, and 2 cups of water, and blend on high until smooth. Season to taste with salt, then pour the puree into the pot with the butternut squash and potato. Increase the heat to medium, cover, and cook until the vegetables are tender, 25 to 30 minutes. Season to taste with salt.
5. To assemble the tortas, slice the bolillos in half lengthwise. Heat a comal, griddle, or large skillet over medium-high heat. Toast the bolillos on both sides until golden. This will add a layer of texture to prevent the tortas from getting too soggy.
6. Spread the mayo on the cut sides of both bolillos. Then add the avocado to each. Smash the avocado with a fork, allowing the mayo and avocado to blend, then season with salt.
7. On the bottom half of each bolillo, arrange the cheese and immediately add the warm squash-and-potato mixture. Sprinkle on the onions and close the tortas with the bolillo tops.

Vitamina T(ip)

Save any leftover squash colorado, as it makes a delicious filling for flautas, gorditas, or quesadillas.

Steak Cemita Poblana

MAKES 2 TORTAS

- 2 Steak Milanesas (recipe follows)
- 2 cemita buns (or sesame-seed burger buns), split open
- 1 avocado, halved and sliced
- Flaky sea salt, such as Maldon
- 1¼ cups (loosely packed) hand-pulled strands quesillo (a.k.a. queso Oaxaca), or 1 cup shredded low-moisture mozzarella
- 2 tablespoons Chipotle Puree (page 73)
- ¼ small red onion, thinly sliced
- 8 fresh pápalo leaves (optional)

Cemitas are among the rare exceptions that fall outside the otherwise binary bolillo-telera bread framework, relying instead on an egg-rich, challah-like bun coated in sesame seeds that goes by the same name of cemita. If you can't find cemita buns at your local Mexican grocer, let it rip with seeded hamburger buns. Just don't hold back on that cheese, avocado . . . or pápalo. A transportive herb reminiscent of cilantro and Thai basil combined, pápalo electrifies every bite of this torta and is—at least part of—what makes it distinctly poblana (i.e., from the state of Puebla). If you can't find pápalo fresh, just leave it out—there's really no substitute.

Place a steak milanesa on the bottom half of each cemita. Top with the avocado and season with a little bit of flaky sea salt. Add a heap of cheese (don't worry about keeping the cheese contained; it's okay if some peeks out of the bread). Drizzle on a tablespoon of the chipotle puree (or less if you prefer it less spicy), followed by the onion and pápalo leaves (if using). Close the tortas with the cemita tops and enjoy.

Steak Milanesas

Steak Milanesa (Milanese-style steak) refers to a pounded, breaded pan-fried steak. As with the Steak Cemita Poblana (above), we'll be using the milanesas in tortas, but this recipe can be enjoyed as a plato fuerte (main course), too. Serve alongside some Arroz a la Mexicana (page 240), Smoky Refried Beans (page 238), and Escabeche (page 256), for peak comfort. Cooked steak milanesas can be stored in the fridge for 3 to 5 days in an airtight container or plastic wrap. Uncooked, prepped steaks can be stored in the freezer for up to 6 months.

MAKES 2 STEAKS

- ½ cup all-purpose flour
- ¾ teaspoon Morton kosher salt
- ¾ teaspoon freshly ground black pepper
- 2 large eggs
- ½ cup fine dried bread crumbs (such as Progresso)
- Neutral oil
- 2 thin pieces of top round steak (4 ounces each)

1. Set up a dredging station in 3 shallow bowls: Pour the flour, salt, and pepper into one bowl and mix well. Crack the eggs into the second bowl and lightly whisk. Pour the bread crumbs into the third bowl.
2. Pour about ½ inch of oil into a large skillet and heat over medium heat until very hot but not smoking. Line a plate with paper towels and keep near the stove.
3. While the oil heats, pound the steak pieces to a ½-inch thickness. Working with one piece at a time, dip it into the seasoned flour to lightly coat each side, then into the beaten egg, then into the bread crumbs, turning to coat both sides. Place the breaded steak on a plate and repeat with the second piece.
4. Pan-fry the steaks until golden brown on both sides, 1½ to 2 minutes per side. (Depending on the size of your pan, you may have to do this one piece at a time.) Transfer the steaks to the paper towels to drain. Keep warm until ready to use.

NARANJA

"Payo Especial" Torta

MAKES 1 INSANELY HUGE TORTA

- 8 guajillo chiles, stemmed, seeded, and veins removed
- 2 cascabel chiles, stemmed and seeded
- ¼ cup neutral oil, plus more for frying
- 3 garlic cloves, peeled
- ½ cup cilantro (leaves and tender stems)
- ⅓ cup roughly chopped red onion (about ¼ onion)
- 3½ teaspoons Chipotle Puree (page 73)
- Kosher salt
- 10 ounces boneless pork loin, cut into ¼-inch-thick slices
- ½ cups grated Mexican Manchego cheese (a.k.a. quesadilla cheese) or queso Chihuahua
- 1 bolillo, homemade (page 57) or store-bought
- ¼ cup lime mayonnaise (preferably McCormick or homemade, page 30)
- 2 thick-cut slices deli ham (2½ ounces)
- 2 tablespoons yellow mustard
- ½ avocado, sliced
- 1 medium ripe tomato, sliced
- ¼ medium white onion, thinly sliced
- 1 serrano chile, stemmed and thinly sliced

Special Equipment

Blender

Still me, Fermín, here to share that El Payo in Torreón is one of those spots that's been named after the character who makes the place what it is. In other words, Payo himself is the place, and the place is Payo, you get me? If you've ever met Payo, you'll know there's nothing he enjoys more than entertaining and delighting his customers. His love for what he does is infectious, and it serves as a constant inspiration for me when it comes to my own restaurants. Of note, the pork adobada here is fried, unlike that in the Pork Adobada "del Beis" Torta (page 73), making this a bit more naughty (the double shot of mayo doesn't hurt). Taking one of these down is like eating a giant Texas BBQ lunch; you can probably count on skipping dinner afterward.

1. In a large bowl, combine the guajillo and cascabel chiles and enough hot water to cover. Soak the chiles until soft, about 10 minutes.

2. Meanwhile, in a medium sauté pan over medium-high heat, warm the oil. Add the garlic and cook, stirring occasionally, until soft and golden brown all over, about 8 minutes. Drain the chiles, reserving some of their soaking liquid. In a blender, combine the chiles, the fried garlic and its cooking oil, the cilantro, red onion, and chipotle puree and blend until it forms a smooth, thick adobo paste. Add a bit of the reserved soaking liquid from the chiles as needed to keep the blender moving. Season to taste with salt.

3. In a medium bowl, lightly salt the pork all over. Rub the pork with the adobo paste, cover, and marinate in the fridge for 25 minutes or up to overnight.

4. Set a medium cast-iron skillet over medium heat. Coat with about ½ inch of oil, or enough for the pork to be fully submerged. Pan-fry the pork adobada until golden, about 4 minutes per piece. (Depending on the size of your pan, you might need to do this in multiple batches.) Chop the pork into bite-size pieces and keep warm.

5. Wipe out the skillet and set it over medium heat. To create a costra, or cheese "crust," add the cheese to the pan and allow it to melt slowly and spread out. While this is happening, slice the bolillo in half lengthwise and spread 1 tablespoon of the mayo evenly on the top half and 1 tablespoon on the bottom half. When the edges of the cheese start to take on some color, about 5 minutes, place the top bolillo half in the pan, mayo-side down. This will allow the cheese and bread to get to know each other and form a bond that can be broken only with one's mouth upon consumption. After 2 minutes, using a metal spatula, remove the bread with its costra from the pan and set aside. Toast the bottom half, mayo-side down, until golden-brown, then remove from the pan and set aside.

6. In the same skillet over medium heat, sear the ham until browned a bit, 2 minutes on each side.

7. On the bottom half of the bolillo, evenly spread the remaining mayo and the mustard. Next, add the avocado and smash it with a fork, spreading it over the bun, then season with salt. Top the avocado with the chopped pork, followed by the seared ham, the tomato, onion, and serrano. Close the torta with the cheesy bolillo top.

Brisket “de la Barda” Torta

MAKES 2 TORTAS

- 2 bolillos, homemade (page 57) or store-bought
- ¼ cup Smoky Refried Beans (page 238, made with black beans), warmed
- 4 thin slices deli ham
- 4 slices American cheese
- ½ cup (3 ounces) Chorizo Rojo (page 237)
- ½ medium white onion, finely diced
- ½ medium ripe tomato, finely diced
- ½ avocado, sliced
- 4 thin slices head cheese (or more deli ham)
- 1 cup (5 ounces) Pulled Brisket (recipe follows)
- Salsa de Chicharrón (page 248), for serving
- Escabeche, homemade (page 256) or store-bought, for serving

This “de la Barda” is the torta equivalent of the Meat Lover’s Pizza, if we’ve ever seen one, calling on not two, not three, but *four* (count ’em!) meats and a meat salsa to boot. This torta hails from Tampico, a port city in the state of Tamaulipas. Its name comes from the barda, or “brick wall,” of the Tampico Marine Terminal, along which several torterías have set up shop since the 1930s, serving the eponymous dish.

1. Slice the bolillos in half lengthwise, making sure to not cut all the way through (they should look like hot dog buns, rather than separated halves).
2. Spread the refried beans on each bottom half. Dividing evenly, top with the ham, American cheese, chorizo, onion, tomato, avocado, head cheese, and pulled brisket. Close the tortas with the bolillo tops. Serve with the salsa de chicharrón and escabeche on the side.

Pulled Brisket

Use the pulled brisket (carne deshebrada) in the Beef Salpicón Tostadas (page 35) or in the Brisket “de la Barda” Torta (above).

MAKES 1½ POUNDS

- 2 pounds fatty brisket, cut into 2 equal pieces
- 1 medium onion, unpeeled, halved through the root end
- 1 head of garlic, halved horizontally
- 4 bay leaves
- 3 tablespoons Morton kosher salt
- 1 tablespoon black peppercorns

1. In a Dutch oven or large, heavy pot, combine the brisket, onion, garlic, bay leaves, salt, and peppercorns, then add enough water to cover the brisket by 2½ to 3 inches. Bring to a boil over medium-high heat. Reduce to a simmer, cover, and cook until the meat is tender, 2 to 2½ hours.
2. Allow the brisket to cool in the pot for 20 minutes, then remove it from the liquid. (Pro tip: Strain the liquid, store it in an airtight container in the fridge, and reserve it for use as a base for future braises, soups, or stews.)
3. Remove the fat cap from the brisket, if necessary, and discard. Using your hands or 2 forks, thoroughly shred the brisket. Store the pulled brisket in an airtight container in the fridge for 4 to 6 days or up to 1 month in the freezer.

Torta Ahogada

MAKES 2 TORTAS

- 2 ripe Roma (plum) tomatoes, quartered
- 2 garlic cloves, peeled
- ½ medium onion, roughly chopped
- 1 red Fresno chile, stemmed and seeded
- 1 tablespoon dried Mexican oregano
- 1 bay leaf
- 6 tablespoons neutral oil
- Kosher salt
- 2 mini baguettes (6 inches long), or 2 (6-inch) lengths cut from a regular baguette
- ½ cup Smoky Refried Beans (page 238, made with pinto beans), warmed
- 1⅓ cups (6 ounces) Surtido Carnitas (page 109)
- Habanero-Pickled Onions (page 257), for serving

Special Equipment

Blender

Ahogadas are relatively light on the filling count but heavy on the zhuzh. Ahogar means "to drown," as in, "Let's drown these tortas in some jueje." In this case, the zhuzh typically consists of two elements: a basic tomato sauce and a chile de árbol salsa. To lighten the prep a bit without sacrificing flavor, we went for a single Fresno-infused tomato sauce. You'll also notice that this iconic torta from Guadalajara calls for birotes—which are mini sourdough baguettes (you can find them in the frozen aisle at Trader Joe's or Central Market)—but a basic baguette will also do just fine.

1. In a blender, combine the tomatoes, garlic, onion, chile, oregano, bay leaf, and 1 cup of water, and blend until smooth.
2. In a medium-to-large saucepan over high heat, warm the oil until it starts to smoke. Carefully pour in the blended sauce and stir constantly to ensure the bottom of the pot doesn't scorch. (The bigger the pot the better, to prevent the sauce from spilling over or splattering.) When the sauce has boiled for 2 minutes, reduce the heat to a simmer and cook for 20 minutes (the sauce will deepen in color). Season to taste with salt, cover, and set aside. (If you're preparing the sauce ahead of time, make sure to warm it before use.)
3. Toast the baguettes in a toaster oven or a 350°F oven for 5 minutes, or until the crust is hard but not burnt.
4. Cut each baguette in half and lightly spread the refried pinto beans on both halves of each. On the bottom half of each baguette, add the carnitas, sandwich the halves together, and place them on their own plates. Pour the warm tomato sauce over each torta to submerge it and surround it with a pool of sauce. Serve with the pickled onions on the side.

Torta Ahogada (page 83)

Concha with Nata

MAKES 4 TORTAS

¾ cup heavy cream

¼ cup confectioners' sugar

¼ cup Mexican crema

4 Vanilla Conchas (page 226)

Special Equipment

Electric hand mixer (optional)

We couldn't do a chapter on tortas without including a riff on this sweet sammie classic served at the finest fondas throughout Mexico. The original is made on the Mexican sweet bread called concha and it is filled with nata—boiled, unpasteurized milk similar in flavor and texture to clotted cream and mascarpone. Widely available in Mexico, nata is less common at U.S. grocers, but we think this homemade hack—which is not technically nata in the strictest sense—gets us pretty close. We add a dash of Mexican crema to freshly whipped cream for a hint of acidity and textural weight. Additional fillings, like strawberries, honey, and/or shaved chocolate, are welcome pairings if your sweet tooth still comes calling.

1 In a medium metal bowl, combine the cream and confectioners' sugar. Using a handheld whisk or an electric hand mixer set on high speed, whisk constantly and vigorously until the cream starts to expand in size and creates soft peaks, about 4 minutes. Using a spatula, fold in the crema.

2 Slice the conchas in half horizontally. On a comal, griddle, or large skillet over medium heat, toast the insides of the conchas until golden, 1 to 2 minutes, then remove from the heat and fill with the whipped cream.

TACOS

Not just a noun but also a verb

Let’s be real: A lot of information on the subject of tacos has been around since well before this cookbook ever existed.

In addition to numerous outstanding cookbooks (*Tacos, Tacopedia* . . .), there have been dozens of academic books and articles, television shows, podcasts, newspaper columns, and food festivals dedicated to this beloved staple—and deservedly so. This is all to say that you, a well-traveled, self-proclaimed tacophile, likely already knew a thing or two about tacos before picking up *Vitamina T*. Right?

For instance, you probably already knew that the word taco originally referred to the little hand-wrapped explosives used for excavation in silver-mining communities throughout Mexico in the eighteenth century, or that tacos have arguably been a dish for as long as tortillas have been a thing (i.e., thousands of years), no?

Of course, you definitely already knew what the taco-ready eating position looks like [cue the 45-degree head tilt]; that a hard-shell taco filled with ground beef and shredded cheddar cheese is [*hot take*] as “Mexican” as the taco al pastor at El Huequito; and that taco is not just a noun but also a verb, as in “Okay, but will it taco?”

Yes?

We thought so. No need to reinvent this masa-based wheel with a run-of-the-mill chapter intro here, then. Instead, here’s a poetic primer on the dynamism of tacos, written by one of Fermín’s and my dear friends and colleagues, Hallie Davison, taco evangelist at large.

If you have a tortilla, and load it up with toppings, it is a taco.

Taco

If you double up on tortillas, that's a taco con copia.

If you double up on fillings, like suadero and tripa or bistec and longaniza, it's a campechano.

If you crisp the cheese directly on the comal, it's a costra.

If you sizzle up your protein with onions, peppers, and bacon, and serve tortillas on the side, it's an alambre.

If you sandwich your filling and cheese between two corn tortillas, it's called a mulita.

If you sandwich your filling and cheese between two flour tortillas, it's called a sincronizada.

If you're in Sonora, a carne asada taco with cheese on a flour tortilla is a caramelo.

If you swap the flour tortilla for corn, toast it, and add your toppings, it's a lorenza, but elsewhere it's a vampiro or a volcán.

And that's just the beginning . . . Bueno.

Magic

A taco is not just a taco, is not just a taco, so without further ado, let's taco, friends.

PERFECT YOUR MASA GAME

Mixing masa is part art, part science. To nail the ideal masa texture—moist without sticking to your hands, like fresh Play Doh—follow these tips.

Don't Forget to Hydrate!

Masa harina loves water (we should all aspire to be more like it). While we recommend starting with a 1:1 ratio of masa harina to warm water, you may need to add a bit more water if it feels too dry, or a bit more masa harina if feels too sticky.

Mix, Mix, Mix

Masa doesn't contain gluten, so there's no such thing as over-kneading. Three to five minutes of hand-mixing will help ensure even absorption.

Give It a Rest

Allowing the masa to sit for 15 minutes or so will allow it to fully hydrate. Be sure to cover it with a damp towel.

The Smush Test

If you think your masa is still thirsty, roll a small ball and smush it down with a finger. If the edges crack, it needs more water. If the edges are smooth, press and cook away.

The Slap Test

Check if your masa is too wet by slapping the dough with an open hand. If any masa sticks to your hand, add a pinch more masa harina and continue mixing. If your hand comes up clean, you're good to go.

Vitamina T(ips)

To bring your day-old homemade tortillas (or any store-bought tortillas) back to life, brush each side with a tiny bit of water and warm each side on a hot comal before transferring it to a clean kitchen towel or tortilla warmer. If the tortillas are too stale to resuscitate, don't throw them out! Use them for: enchiladas (see page 221), tostadas (see pages 26 to 29), totopos for chilaquiles (see page 222), tacos dorados (see page 132) . . . the masa-bilities are virtually endless.

Corn Tortillas

MAKES 12 TORTILLAS (5 TO 6 INCHES IN DIAMETER)

1 cup (120g; packed) masa harina, plus more as needed

1 teaspoon Morton kosher salt (optional)

Scant 1 cup (230g) warm (but not hot) water, plus more as needed

Special Equipment

Digital scale; tortilla press and plastic liners; tortilla warmer (optional)

How to Make Corn Tortillas

¡Qué onda! Fermín here, to tell you a little story about tortilla recipes. Back in 2019, Jorge attempted to write a straightforward, one-page recipe for the corn tortilla. Two hundred and seventy-one pages, three years, and one pandemic later, that recipe eventually went on to become the nationally best-selling cookbook better known as *MASA: Techniques, Recipes, and Reflections on a Timeless Staple*. Rest assured, this recipe right here is not *that* recipe. This one is basic in the best of ways, calling for store-bought masa flour (we are partial to Masienda, of course) and only a few minutes of prep. There will be no dried corn, calcium hydroxide, or lava-stone mills in the making of these tortillas, and you can trust us that they'll still be delicious—because that's the only way we know how to make corn tortillas, chef. That said, if you, like us, are also into nixtamalization and corn-nerd things, be sure to check out *MASA*.

1. In a medium bowl, combine the masa harina and salt (if using). Working by hand, mix in the warm water, kneading the dough until the water is fully incorporated and there are no dry spots. Don't worry about overworking the dough—corn has no gluten, so knead to your heart's content. Tortilla masa should be moist to the touch but not tacky (leaving bits of wet dough on your hand and fingers). If it's too wet, add a bit more masa harina; if too dry, add a bit more water.
2. Preheat a comal, griddle, or large skillet over medium-high heat. (Do this now! It's important for the comal to be hot before you start cooking.) Line a tortilla press with 2 plastic liners.
3. Form the masa into balls the size of Ping-Pong balls. You should wind up with about 12 equal balls (about 30g each).
4. Using the lined tortilla press, place a ball of masa on the bottom liner, then close the press and apply pressure to flatten the masa. You're looking for a tortilla about 1⁄16 inch thick and 5 to 6 inches in diameter. Open the press and remove the top plastic liner. Place the tortilla on your palm, then remove the bottom plastic liner.
5. On the comal over medium-high heat, gently lay the tortilla down in a smooth, backhanded motion (this move takes some practice but is the best way to ensure your tortillas lay down flat without folding). Sear the first side of the tortilla for 25 to 30 seconds, until the edges begin to change color slightly, then use a spatula or your bare hands to flip and cook the other side for 25 to 30 seconds.
6. Flip the tortilla once more and cook for 10 to 20 more seconds—if the stars are aligned, this is when you'll get a tortilla puff! Your tortilla will be delicious no matter what, but it sure is a crowd-pleaser when you get that magic puff. Keep practicing and it'll happen.
7. Wrap the cooked tortilla inside a clean kitchen towel or place in a tortilla warmer. Repeat with the rest of the dough balls, reusing the same plastic liners. Scan the QR code to see how it's done.

Fermín's Flour Tortillas

MAKES 12 TORTILLAS (6 TO 7 INCHES IN DIAMETER)

1¼ cups (310g) whole milk

2 tablespoons unsalted butter

Neutral oil

3⅓ cups (425g) all-purpose flour, plus more for dusting

2 teaspoons baking powder

2 teaspoons Morton kosher salt

Special Equipment

Digital scale; rolling pin

How to Make Flour Tortillas

Being from the north of Mexico, Torreón to be exact, Fermín has always had some kind of flour tortilla recipe in his back pocket for any and all occasions. This one is simple but dynamic, allowing for any range of fats to be substituted for the butter and/or oil in equal measure; just don't touch that milk, as it's what gives these tortillas their ever-so-subtle sweetness. If you're looking for a Sonora-style flour tortilla—the translucent kind that comes with a higher fat-to-flour ratio and is considerably thinner in size—this ain't it. Properly executed, these should be pillowy in texture with just the right amount of fatty flakiness that doesn't steal the show from your toppings.

1. In a small saucepan over medium-low heat, combine the milk, butter, and 2½ tablespoons of oil and heat until the mixture is warm to the touch. Do not allow the milk to boil or scald. (You may need to take the mixture off the heat before the butter is fully incorporated and allow it to melt in the residual heat.)
2. In a large bowl, combine the flour, baking powder, and salt. Make a well in the center of the dry mixture. Pour the warmed milk mixture into the well. Using a rubber spatula and/or your hands, fold the dry ingredients into the wet ingredients until just combined. The dough should look shaggy and feel tacky to the touch. Be careful not to overwork the dough, as it will yield a tough tortilla.
3. Lightly oil the inside of another large bowl and place the ball of dough inside; turn to coat lightly with oil. Cover the bowl with plastic wrap and allow it to rest in the fridge for 30 minutes.
4. Remove the dough from the fridge and divide it evenly into 12 pieces (about 60g each). Roll each piece into a rough ball shape, taking care not to overwork the dough. Place the portioned dough balls on a plate or a sheet pan and cover with a damp towel. Let rest for 15 more minutes.
5. Preheat a lightly oiled comal, griddle, or large skillet over medium-high heat.
6. Remove the towel and dust the dough balls with plenty of flour—enough to cover the tops of the dough. Using a rolling pin dusted with flour and working with one ball at a time, roll out the dough ball into a circle 6 to 7 inches in diameter (don't worry if it isn't perfectly round). You may choose to roll out one tortilla and then cook it, repeating for each remaining ball, or you can roll the balls all out at once and place them between sheets of parchment before cooking.
7. Place a tortilla on the hot comal and cook until the surface of the tortilla becomes opaque, bubbles begin to form, and the edges begin to pull up from the comal, about 30 seconds. Flip and cook the second side for about 20 more seconds. Remove the tortilla from the comal and wrap it in a clean kitchen towel. Repeat with the remaining tortillas. Scan the QR code to see how it's done.

Al Pastor Tacos

MAKES 16 TO 20 TACOS

Adobo

- 10 guajillo chiles, stemmed, seeded, and veins removed
- 5 dried puya (pulla) chiles, stemmed, seeded, and veins removed
- 1 medium onion, roughly chopped
- 1 cup apple cider vinegar
- 5 garlic cloves, peeled
- 2 tablespoons Morton kosher salt
- 1 tablespoon dried Mexican oregano

Al Pastor

- Kosher salt
- 2 pounds boneless pork shoulder or butt, cut into 1-inch-thick slices
- 4 ounces thinly sliced bacon, cut into 2-inch lengths
- Neutral oil

Tacos

- 16 to 20 corn tortillas, homemade (page 97) or store-bought, warmed
- 1 cup fresh pineapple chunks (about ¼ medium)
- Minced cilantro, for garnish
- Finely diced white onion, for garnish
- Salsa Verde Cruda (page 249) and/or Salsa Roja (page 244), for serving

Special Equipment

- Blender; charcoal or gas grill or grill pan

There are a few technical factors (see page 104) that give professional tacos al pastor—cooked on and deftly carved from a trompo (vertical spit)—a slight edge over homemade, trompo-less tacos al pastor, but that didn't stop us from getting deliciously close. The trick here is to slice the pork shoulder so as to mimic the extended surface area that the trompo exposes to direct heat. This translates to more char per square bite, and an even tastier char if using good old-fashioned charcoal, which we always recommend.

1. **Make the adobo:** In a medium saucepan, combine the guajillo chiles, puya chiles, onion, vinegar, garlic, salt, and oregano. Add just enough water to cover all the ingredients. Bring to a boil over medium-high heat. Reduce the heat and simmer until the chiles, onion, and garlic are soft, about 45 minutes. Remove from the heat and let cool.
2. Transfer the chile mixture to a blender along with all of the liquid from the pan and blend on medium-high until smooth.
3. **Make the al pastor:** Lightly salt the sliced pork and let rest for 10 minutes. In a large bowl, combine the pork and bacon. Pour the adobo over the meat. Cover the bowl with plastic wrap and refrigerate for at least 2 hours or preferably overnight.
4. Prepare a charcoal or gas grill for high heat. Clean the grates well and brush them with oil. (Alternatively, preheat a grill pan over medium-high heat and brush the pan with oil.) Grill the marinated pork and bacon over direct heat until well done, about 5 minutes per side for the pork and 3 minutes per side for the bacon. (Careful: the fatty bacon will likely catch fire on the grill.)
5. Remove the pork and bacon to a cutting board and chop together into thin strips.
6. **Assemble the tacos:** Top each tortilla with the chopped meat, the pineapple, cilantro, and onion, then serve with your choice of salsa.

Vitamina T(ip)

This adobo is great not only for pork but also for grilled fish, shrimp, chicken, etc. You may consider doubling the recipe and freezing some for future use on whatever your heart desires.

Tacos al Pastor

Can one of Mexico's most iconic tacos, which was inspired by Middle Eastern immigrants and is only a few decades old, still be considered "authentically" or "traditionally" Mexican? If a tree falls in a forest and no one is there to hear it, does it make a sound? Obviously, yes on both counts. To be sure, few seem to question the Mexicanity of tacos al pastor—we certainly don't—but it serves as a friendly reminder to embrace the changing face of what it means to be "Mexican."

AL PASTOR GUIDE

All hail [*one of*] the greatest of all tacos (G.O.A.T.)! Okay, now that you know how we really feel about tacos al pastor, we present a short field guide to identifying excellent tacos al pastor in the wild.

Luck of the trompo

Brand-new trompo fresh out the gates? Maybe keep walking. Even the best-composed trompos require some time to char, render, and crisp evenly along the exterior. Be patient and still, our beating hearts.

Carne laminada

As pictured, great al pastor meat has a sheeted, laminated finish when thinly (i.e., deftly) sliced. This is usually a solid indication that the trompo has had ample time to properly marinate and fuse. A thin slice's subtle translucence is an added indication that the meat was desirably cooked.

Carving technique

A taquero who holds a tortilla close to the meat being carved is a good sign, as it most likely means it's been cooked perfectly enough to hit the tortilla directly, without further interference on a plancha.

Flair

How does the taquero's technique look? Extra points for how theatrically they cut the pineapple garnish.

Color

Too much red is a red flag. This usually indicates it is more about the marinade than the pork, and we're looking for harmony here.

Got masa?

Freshly pressed tortillas are always a plus and worth the upsell. Trust.

Carnitas Tacos

MAKES 15 TO 20 TACOS

- 15 to 20 corn tortillas, homemade (page 97) or store-bought, warmed
- Surtido Carnitas (page 109)

Garnishes

- Pico de Gallo (page 253)
- Salsa Verde Cruda (page 249)
- Lime wedges, for squeezing
- Escabeche, homemade (page 256) or store-bought

The traditional texture of carnitas is tender, succulent, melt-in-your-mouth, and Fermín is partial to these tacos with their straight-out-of-the-olla (pot) doneness level for the carnitas. If you're looking for a bit more bite, however, you can always reheat the meat in a skillet for some caramelization (a.k.a. doradita).

Top each tortilla with a generous portion of the carnitas and add the pico de gallo, salsa cruda, a squeeze of lime, and the escabeche.

RECIPE CONTINUES →

CHORIZO
FLAUTAS
SUADERO

Radial
All
Coca-Cola

Surtido Carnitas

MAKES 3½ POUNDS

10 cups lard (about 4 pounds)

Kosher salt

3 pounds boneless pork shoulder, cut into roughly 4-inch cubes

1 pound pork belly (preferably skin-on), cut into 2-inch cubes

1 pig's trotter (optional)

1 cup warm (but not hot) water

1 medium onion, quartered

1 head of garlic, halved horizontally

1 bay leaf

1 cinnamon stick (preferably Mexican canela)

Juice of 1 sour orange, or 1 navel orange and 2 limes

8 ounces pig skin

Special Equipment

Candy/deep-fry thermometer

When it comes to carnitas—pork slowly cooked in its own fat—pork shoulder (maciza) tends to be the crowd-pleasing cut of choice for most mainstream recipes out there in the world. And hey, that's cool. Pork shoulder is delicious, and we're not in the business of yucking anyone's yum. *But,* if you've ever enjoyed truly exceptional carnitas in Mexico, odds are that your bites were of the surtido—or assorted cuts—persuasion, and that's what we're gathered here to cook today. Surtido can be any combination of meat, especially offal and fat, so feel free to improvise in this recipe if you'd like . . . or maybe just trust us on this one?

1. Clip a candy/deep-fry thermometer to the side of a large Dutch oven or large, heavy pot and heat the lard over medium-high heat until it reaches 400°F. (This can take up to 20 minutes.)
2. Meanwhile, lightly salt the pork shoulder and pork belly, keeping them separate, and allow to come to room temperature.
3. When the lard reaches 400°F, using a heat-resistant mitt and tongs, carefully place the pork shoulder in the hot lard and sear the outside of the meat. Continue cooking the pork in the lard until the temperature registers 400°F again, about 15 minutes.
4. Carefully add the pork belly to the pot and cook for 15 minutes. Reduce the heat to medium-low to bring the lard to a gentle simmer. Add the trotter (if using) and cook for 1 hour.
5. Just before the hour is up, dissolve 1½ tablespoons of salt in the warm water. When the hour is up, carefully add the salted water, the onion, garlic, bay leaf, cinnamon stick, sour orange juice, and pig skin to the pot. Cover and continue to cook over low heat, enough to keep the lard simmering, until meat is tender, about 1½ hours. Allow the lard to cool slightly. (To save and reuse the lard for future cooking purposes, strain it through a fine-mesh strainer and discard the remaining solids. Store in an airtight container in the fridge for up to 1 year.)
6. Place a wire rack on a sheet pan. Remove the meat (including the pig skin) from the pot and place it on the rack to drain. Take the trotter (if using) and remove as much meat as you can from the bone, then add to the wire rack. On a cutting board, coarsely chop all the meat together using a sharp knife or meat cleaver. Store the carnitas in an airtight container in the fridge for 3 to 5 days.

Brisket Suadero Tacos

MAKES 16 TO 18 TACOS

16 to 18 corn tortillas, homemade (page 97) or store-bought, warmed

Brisket Suadero (recipe follows), warmed

Garnishes

Minced cilantro

Diced white onion

Thickly sliced radishes

Thickly sliced cucumbers

Salsa Verde (page 245)

Salsa Roja (page 244)

Spring onions (reserved from Brisket Suadero)

You didn't hear it from me (Jorge), but suadero is one of Fermín's favorite tacos. Believe it or not, I think he'd name his first child Suadero. Fermín's been working on variations of suadero for a minute, and he believes that this confit, slow-cook method is the only way to get this dish right. A slow, extended cook allows a traditionally tough cut of meat to fully break down and become luxuriously tender. If you've ever had suadero in the wild, you've probably noticed the meat is poached in a hot-fat Jacuzzi of sorts, also known as a chorizera or discada. A chorizera looks like a metal comal, or pan, with a raised convex center and circular trough that runs around its circumference. The tortillas are cooked at a higher temperature atop the chorizera's raised dome, while the meat slowly bathes in fat at a much lower temperature on the trough side—hence our Dutch oven fat-poaching method.

Top each tortilla with about 1 ounce (about 2 tablespoons) of the brisket suadero and garnish with the cilantro, onion, radishes, and cucumbers, then drizzle with the salsa verde and salsa roja. Serve with the spring onions on the side.

Brisket Suadero

True suadero (a.k.a. "rose meat") can be difficult to source in the United States, so we've opted for brisket here, which imparts the same beefy flavor and has a slightly heartier texture.

MAKES 1½ POUNDS

2 pounds fatty brisket, cut into 4 pieces

Kosher salt

8 cups beef tallow or lard (about 4 pounds)

1 bunch of spring onions (a.k.a. cambray onions), trimmed

1. Preheat the oven to 250°F.
2. Score the meat on all sides, making shallow cuts across the surface in a diagonal pattern to create a crosshatch design, which allows the salt to penetrate. Liberally salt the brisket on all sides.
3. In a Dutch oven or large, heavy pot over low heat, warm the tallow to liquefy the fat. When the fat is melted, add the brisket and spring onions. Cover and transfer the pot to the oven. Bake until the meat is tender, about 4½ hours.
4. Remove the meat from the pot and chop with a cleaver to mix the fattier part with the lean. Remove the spring onions and set aside for serving the tacos. (If you wish to save and reuse the tallow for future cooking purposes, strain it through a fine-mesh strainer and discard the remaining solids. Store the tallow in an airtight container in the fridge for up to 1 year.) Store the suadero in airtight container for 4 to 6 days or up to 1 month in the freezer.

Tacos Campechanos

MAKES 16 TO 18 TACOS

1 cup (8 ounces) Chorizo Rojo (page 237), warmed

1 cup (8 ounces) Brisket Suadero (page 110), warmed

16 to 18 corn tortillas, homemade (page 97) or store-bought, warmed

Garnishes

Minced cilantro

Diced white onion

Salsa Verde Cruda (page 249)

Salsa Roja (page 244)

Do you get anxious when ordering food? Have you or a loved one ever experienced decision paralysis when choosing between a suadero taco (see page 110) and a tripas taco (see page 114)? Do you suffer from Taco FOMO? Introducing . . . campechano, the taco that's not interested in "either" and "or" because—why not just *both*? To campechanear is "to mix," in Mexico, and there's really no limit to just how you bring that mix to life. Well, *almost* none. No one would ever dare make a campechano with al pastor (see page 101), for some unspoken reason, but we've got plenty of other options bubbling in the chorizera, or discada (a sort of meat Jacuzzi) to keep everyone happy. Speaking of joy, Fermín gets especially ebullient about the suadero/chorizo combo for its fatty/spicy balance, so yeah, that's the inspo for this particular mix right here, in case you were wondering.

1. On a cutting board, combine the chorizo and suadero. Chop them together with a cleaver until well mixed.
2. Place the mixture on the tortillas and garnish with the cilantro, onion, and salsas.

Tripas Tacos

MAKES 12 TACOS

- 5 pounds precleaned beef intestines (tripas), purchased from a reputable source
- Kosher salt
- 1 medium onion, unpeeled, quartered
- 1 head of garlic, halved horizontally
- 6 tablespoons lard or olive oil
- 12 corn tortillas, homemade (page 97) or store-bought, warmed

Garnishes

- Minced cilantro
- Diced white onion
- Salsa de Chile de Árbol (page 250) or Salsa de Molcajete (page 251)

We know that you know how good this taco looks. We think so, too. We also know that some of you wouldn't just write off this taco once you discovered that tripas means "tripe"—because that wouldn't be cool. Plus, this taco really tastes as good as it looks, and that's coming from two people who are not exactly offal lovers themselves. If you're still having a hard time with the name or the concept, remember that this recipe calls for the small intestines, not honeycomb tripe; and we zealously believe that this distinction is the platonic ideal (in all seriousness!). The small intestines have a meatier quality to them and balanced fat, which, when lovingly rendered, yields an honest-to-goodness crispy, bacon-bit texture and a clean beefy flavor that most carnivores can't get enough of. Nevertheless, it is crucial to this dish—and for the sake of the smell in your home kitchen—that you source your tripas from a reputable purveyor that offers them precleaned.

1. Using a sharp knife or kitchen scissors, trim as much fat from the outside of the tripas as possible (it's okay if a small amount remains).
2. In a large soup pot, combine the tripas with water to cover by 5 inches. Salt the water as aggressively as you would for pasta water. Bring to a boil over medium-high heat and cook at a rolling boil for 1 hour, skimming and discarding the impurities that float to the top.
3. Drain the tripas. Clean the pot and return the tripas to the pot along with the onion and garlic. Again, fill the pot with water to cover the ingredients by 4 to 5 inches and salt the water as aggressively as you would for pasta water. Bring to a boil over medium-high heat, then reduce the heat to low and simmer for 1½ hours, until the tripas are a little firm but break apart fairly easily when pierced with a fork. Let cool in their cooking liquid.
4. When cooled, drain the tripas and cut into rings about ½ inch wide. Rinse under cold running water to remove any impurities. Repeat this rinsing three or four times until the water runs clear. Drain well and pat dry.
5. Set a large cast-iron skillet over medium-high heat and add the lard. When the lard has melted and is hot, add the tripas. As they start to sizzle, stir occasionally, preferably with a slotted spoon. After 2 or 3 minutes, the tripas will start to release fat, which may begin to foam; this is a sign they're on their way to achieving major crispness. Keep stirring constantly until the tripas are golden brown on all sides, 10 to 12 minutes.
6. Using a slotted spoon so the fat drains off, transfer the tripas to a plate. You should end up with about 1 pound of tripas.
7. To serve, top the tortillas with the tripas and garnish with the cilantro, onion, and your salsa of choice.

Barbacoa Tacos

MAKES 16 TACOS

- Kosher salt
- 1 rack of goat ribs with loin attached, cut in half (see Tip)
- ½ medium onion, quartered
- 4 garlic cloves, peeled
- 4 bay leaves
- 4 dried avocado leaves
- 6 tablespoons neutral oil
- 1 maguey leaf, cut in half crosswise, or 2 banana leaves
- 16 corn tortillas, homemade (page 97) or store-bought, warmed

Garnishes

- Salsa Verde Cruda (page 249)
- Minced cilantro
- Diced white onion
- Salsa de Molcajete (page 251)
- Lime wedges, for squeezing

Special Equipment

- Blender

Goat and maguey leaves pair divinely, but we know these ingredients are not the easiest to find. True story: Our culinary team on this cookbook shoot couldn't obtain either ingredient from their fancy restaurant distributors, almost resulting in lamb being subbed for the goat and *maybe* one or two maguey leaves being "foraged" from a public park in downtown LA, using machetes in broad daylight. *Anyways*, barbacoa is perhaps one of the most beautiful and dramatic dishes to behold in Mexico, as it traditionally involves wrapping meat in maguey leaves and cooking it underground for several hours. Talk about a slow reveal! This can be a challenge, if not an impossibility, for most everyone reading this, so rest assured: It has been adapted with the home kitchen in mind. And don't worry; in addition to subbing out the goat for lamb or another accessible protein of your choice, you can use banana leaves instead of maguey leaves, with great success.

1. Preheat the oven to 300°F. Salt the ribs and set aside.
2. In a blender, combine the onion, garlic, bay leaves, avocado leaves, and oil, then blend on medium-high until smooth. Rub the marinade over the ribs on both sides.
3. Wrap the ribs in the maguey leaf by placing one leaf half on the bottom of the ribs and the other leaf half on top, then wrapping in foil to keep the leaf securely in place. (If the meat is too large or difficult to wrap with a single maguey leaf, use 2 banana leaves, following the same method, or as many as needed to fully wrap the rack, then wrap in foil.) Place the meat in a 9 × 13-inch baking dish.
4. Roast until the goat meat is very tender, 3½ to 4 hours. Remove from the oven and let cool, still wrapped.
5. When the ribs are cool enough to handle, unwrap and remove the meat from the bones and transfer to a bowl or serving dish. Discard the bones along with any tough gristle or tendons. Strain the meat's juices into a bowl for use as an accompanying consomé.
6. To serve, top each tortilla with the barbacoa. Garnish with the salsa cruda, cilantro, onion, and salsa de molcajete, then add a squeeze of lime. Serve with the consomé on the side to dunk the tacos into, like a French dip.

Vitamina T(ip)

If you can't find goat, you can substitute 3 lamb necks or 4 pounds of beef cheek. Roast the lamb neck for 5 to 6 hours or the beef cheek for 3½ to 4 hours.

Lengua Tacos

MAKES 20 TACOS

4 pasilla chiles, stemmed, seeded, and veins removed

2 morita chiles, stemmed and seeded

1 tablespoon dried Mexican oregano

2 tablespoons Morton kosher salt

1 beef tongue (3 to 4 pounds)

1 medium onion, thinly sliced

20 corn tortillas, homemade (page 97) or store-bought, warmed

Garnishes

Salsa Verde Cruda (page 249)

Minced cilantro

Diced white onion

Lime wedges, for squeezing

Special Equipment

Blender; tamalera (tamal steamer) or large pot with steamer basket/insert

Like most off-cuts of meat, lengua (beef tongue) can sometimes take a bit more prep or cooking time to alchemize into the gourmet gold that it is, but that's what skilled cooking is all about sometimes. Lengua is a highly satisfying dish made all the more so when sliced lengthwise and thin, as done here and at least one of our CDMX faves, Tacos Tony. As lengua is a richly flavorful cut of meat, it benefits from a brightly acidic salsa like the salsa cruda we have called for here. Give it a whirl, and see just how fun it is to take lengua from French kiss to chef's kiss. (Fermín is disapprovingly shaking his head at that dad joke right now, but Jorge has no regrets.)

1. Preheat a comal or cast-iron skillet over high heat. When hot, toast the pasilla and morita chiles until fragrant and beginning to puff, turning to ensure they don't burn. Remove from the heat as they finish toasting.
2. In a blender, combine the toasted chiles and the oregano, then blend on high until you achieve a powder consistency. Place the powder in a small bowl and stir in the salt. Set this seasoning spice aside. Place the beef tongue on a sheet pan and use a small paring knife to poke holes through the tough outer skin. This will allow the seasoning to penetrate deeper into the meat. Rub the seasoning spice onto the tongue, making sure to get it into the crevices and poked holes.
3. Put a clean penny at the bottom of a tamalera or a pot with a steamer basket/insert, then fill the pot with water and set the steamer insert inside. Line the steamer insert with the onion slices and place the beef tongue on top. Cover and steam over medium heat until the meat is tender and pulls apart easily with a fork, about 3 hours. You'll know if the water level is getting low when the penny starts to make a rattling sound, indicating that more water is needed.
4. Remove the tongue from the pot and let rest until cool enough to handle. Using a sharp knife, cut just under the tongue's outer layer of tough skin and peel it off by hand. Cut the tongue into slices ¼ inch thick.
5. To serve, top each tortilla with 1 to 3 slices of tongue (1 for the thicker back part of the tongue, 2 to 3 slices as you get closer to the tip of the tongue). Garnish with the salsa, cilantro, onion, and a squeeze of lime.

Hecho en

Baja-Style Fish Tacos

MAKES 8 TACOS

- Neutral oil, for frying
- 1 cup all-purpose flour
- ½ cup masa harina
- 1 tablespoon Morton kosher salt, plus more as needed
- 1½ teaspoons baking powder
- 1 (12-ounce) bottle or can lager beer (1½ cups)
- ¼ cup yellow mustard
- 1 pound halibut fillet, cut into 8 strips 3 × 1 inch in size
- 8 corn tortillas, homemade (page 97) or store-bought, warmed

Garnishes

- Chipotle Mayo (page 253)
- ½ head of green cabbage, cored and thinly sliced
- Pico de Gallo (page 253)
- Lime wedges, for squeezing

Special Equipment

- Candy/deep-fry thermometer (optional)

These tacos de pescado, or Baja fish tacos, are like the chicken milanesa (see page 61) of the sea. As pescado purists, we were reluctant to deviate from the classic pick-up (that's kitchen parlance for "preparation") on this dish, but two minor tweaks felt permissible. First, you'll notice that masa harina makes an appearance because we love the hint of nixtamal flavor it imparts to the batter while simultaneously giving it an airy lift. Second, the yellow mustard dials up the batter's color to an effortless golden tan once fried, and it gives the taco a subtle kiss of acidity like that which you might find in, say, a tartar sauce.

1 Pour 3 inches of oil into a Dutch oven or large, heavy pot and clip a candy/deep-fry thermometer to the inside of the pot. Heat the oil over medium heat until the temperature reaches 350°F. (If you don't have a thermometer, dip the handle of a wooden spoon into the oil; if the oil bubbles around the handle, it's hot enough.) Set a wire rack in a sheet pan and keep near the stove.

2 Meanwhile, in a medium bowl, mix the flour, masa harina, salt, and baking powder. Slowly whisk in the beer and mustard, until the ingredients just come together; be careful not to overmix or the batter will be tough. Cover the bowl and place in the fridge until you are ready to fry the fish.

3 When the oil is ready, season the fish with salt. Remove the batter from the fridge. Working with one piece of fish at a time, dip it into the batter and then drop it into the oil. Fry until golden brown, 4 to 6 minutes. (You can fry 2 pieces at once, but any more than that and they may stick together and/or bring down the temperature of the oil.) With a slotted spoon, remove the fried fish from the oil and place on the wire rack to drain; this will prevent the fish from getting soggy. Repeat with the remaining pieces of fish, allowing the oil to come back to temperature before adding the next piece.

4 Top each tortilla with a smear of chipotle mayo, then top with 1 piece of fish followed by the cabbage, pico de gallo, and a squeeze of lime.

Tacos Gobernador

MAKES 6 TACOS

- ¼ cup (½ stick) unsalted butter
- 1 tablespoon paprika
- ½ small onion, finely diced
- 2 ripe Roma (plum) tomatoes, finely diced
- 1 poblano chile, stemmed, seeded, and finely diced
- 1 serrano chile, stemmed, seeded, and finely diced
- 1 pound large shrimp, peeled and deveined, cut into quarters
- Kosher salt
- Neutral oil
- 6 corn tortillas, homemade (page 97) or store-bought
- 1½ cups (loosely packed) hand-pulled strands quesillo (a.k.a. queso Oaxaca), or 1⅛ cups shredded low-moisture mozzarella
- Salsa Tatemada (page 247), for serving
- Lime wedges, for squeezing

Given the cheese and tortilla folding action happening in this dish, it feels like a bit of a misnomer to call this a taco, but that's not a hill we're about to die on today. The dish was supposedly named gobernador, or governor, because it was created in honor of the governor of Sinaloa by Los Arcos restaurant in Mazatlán in the early '90s. Since then, the dish has spread across Mexico, especially throughout the Baja Peninsula, where flour tortillas can and will make the occasional appearance. We've opted for corn tortillas, but any delicious tortilla will ultimately suffice to make this quesadilla, er . . . taco.

1. In a medium saucepan over medium heat, melt the butter. Add the paprika and cook for 30 seconds, until fragrant. Add the onion, tomatoes, and poblano and serrano chiles and cook, stirring occasionally, until soft, about 5 minutes.
2. Increase the heat to medium-high, add the shrimp, and cook, stirring occasionally, until the shrimp are pink and cooked through, 5 to 7 minutes. Remove from the heat and season to taste with salt.
3. On a lightly oiled comal, griddle, or large skillet over medium heat, warm the tortillas, then top each with about ¼ cup of the cheese. Fold the tortillas in half to create quesadillas. Cook on one side until slightly crisp, then flip and cook until the cheese is melted.
4. Place the folded tacos on plates. Open each taco and fill it with the cooked shrimp. Serve with the salsa tatemada and a squeeze of lime.

Sweet Potato Costra Tacos

MAKES 8 TACOS

- 2 medium sweet potatoes
- 1 garlic clove
- ½ cup full-fat plain yogurt
- ¼ cup crumbled feta cheese
- Olive oil
- 1½ teaspoons Morton kosher salt, plus more as needed
- 8 corn tortillas, homemade (page 97) or store-bought
- Salsa Macha (page 252) or store-bought
- Minced cilantro, for garnish
- Scallions (green parts only), thinly sliced, for garnish

Special Equipment

- Immersion blender

Shout-out to Wes Avila and Guerrilla Tacos for this taco's inspiration. While it takes cues from the food-truck-ternt-restaurant's combo of sweet potato (camote) and feta, it changes things up by turning the sweet potato itself into a seared costra (crust) and liquefies the feta into a yogurt-based crema for a salty, tangy finish.

1. Preheat the oven to 425°F. Line a sheet pan with parchment paper or aluminum foil.
2. Using a fork, pierce the sweet potatoes at various points and place them on the sheet pan. Roast the sweet potatoes until tender, 45 minutes to 1 hour, depending on size. Let cool briefly.
3. Meanwhile, in a medium bowl, combine the garlic, yogurt, feta, 1 tablespoon of olive oil, the salt, and 1 tablespoon of water. Using an immersion blender, puree the mixture until smooth, adding more water as needed to achieve a thick, pourable consistency. Taste and season with more salt as needed.
4. In a large nonstick skillet over medium-high heat, warm 1 tablespoon of olive oil. Cut the sweet potatoes in half lengthwise and carefully scoop 2 heaping tablespoons of the flesh into the pan. Top with a tortilla and press flat with your hand. Reduce the heat to medium-low and cook, checking the sweet potato occasionally to prevent burning. When the sweet potato looks caramelized, about 5 minutes, flip and warm the tortilla side, 1 to 2 minutes, and sprinkle with a pinch of salt on the sweet potato side. Transfer to a plate. Repeat with the remaining sweet potato and tortillas, adding more olive oil to the pan as needed.
5. Top each taco with a drizzle of the yogurt-feta sauce, the salsa macha, and a sprinkle of the cilantro and scallions.

Rib Eye Cachetada Tacos

MAKES 6 TACOS

- Neutral oil
- 1 small onion, halved crosswise and cut into 6 wedges
- 6 Fermín's Flour Tortillas (page 98) or store-bought 6-inch flour tortillas
- ¼ cup melted pork lard, melted butter, or olive oil (optional; see Tips)
- 1 cup (packed) coarsely shredded Gouda cheese
- 6 thin slices rib eye from a Mexican butcher (see Tips)
- Kosher salt and freshly ground black pepper
- Salsa Taquera (page 246), for serving

Cachetada translates literally to "slap." And while this taco's etymological origins are somewhat contested, one bite irrefutably confirms that this dish does slap, indeed. Variations on the theme abound, but this particular rendition was inspired by Cara de Vaca restaurant in Monterrey, Mexico. Here, the rib eye is cut thin enough to make sure there's plenty of luxury to go 'round the table. If your local Mexican grocer or butcher is fresh out of rib eye, you can sub in gaonera, or thinly sliced beef tenderloin.

1. In a skillet over medium-low heat, warm 1 tablespoon of oil. Add the onion and cook, stirring every 2 to 4 minutes, until golden brown (as opposed to fully jammy and caramelized), about 20 minutes.
2. Meanwhile, on a comal, griddle, or large skillet over medium-high heat, warm the tortillas on both sides and set aside. (If using store-bought tortillas, brush each side lightly with some of the melted lard after warming.)
3. On the same comal, drop about a sixth of the shredded Gouda (about 2½ tablespoons) and immediately cover with a warmed tortilla, allowing the cheese to melt and turn into a golden-brown costra, or crust. (Peek at the underside to make sure it's done.) Transfer to a plate and continue with the remaining cheese and tortillas.
4. When the onion is golden brown, transfer it to a bowl or serving dish and then wipe out the skillet. Season the slices of rib eye with salt and pepper to taste. Add about 1 tablespoon of oil to the skillet and warm over medium heat. Add the beef slices to the pan and sear until dark brown on both sides, 1 to 2 minutes total.
5. To assemble the tacos, place the tortillas on plates with the costra side facing up, then top each with a slice of the steak and some onion. Serve with the salsa.

Vitamina T(ips)

You need the fat for brushing only if you are using store-bought tortillas. If you have access to a Mexican butcher, you should be able to buy presliced rib eye. If not, buy 1 pound of rib eye steak and use a sharp knife to slice it lengthwise into 6 thin sheets (or ask your butcher to slice it for you).

La Costeña
JALAPEÑOS
ENTEROS
CONT. NET. 2.8 kg
MASA DRENADA 1.54 kg

Bean and Chorizo Tacos

MAKES 8 TACOS

- 1¾ cups (1 pound) Chorizo Rojo (page 237)
- 2 cups Smoky Refried Beans (page 238, made with black beans)
- Kosher salt
- 8 Fermín's Flour Tortillas (page 98) or store-bought 6-inch flour tortillas
- Salsa de Chicharrón (page 248), for serving

You could insist on calling this a mini burrito in taco disguise, and that'd be fine by us. To be sure, however, frijoles con chorizo is a common Norteño taco served on an extra-thin flour tortilla. As you've probably gathered by now, we're rather obsessed with corn masa and corn tortillas, but we do appreciate how much more forgiving flour tortillas can be when it comes to to-go tacos. To this end, this taco is a perfect companion on your next road trip or plane ride, or for some day's desk lunch. Just be sure to pack enough to share.

1. In a medium saucepan over medium heat, warm the chorizo. Add the beans and stir to create a homogeneous mixture. When warmed through, taste and season with salt as needed, then set aside.
2. On a comal, griddle, or large skillet over medium-high heat, warm the tortillas.
3. Top each tortilla with the bean-and-chorizo mixture, and serve with the salsa.

Egg and Machaca Tacos

MAKES 4 TACOS

- Neutral oil
- 4 ounces machaca
- ¼ cup Pico de Gallo (page 253), plus more for garnish
- 4 large eggs
- Kosher salt and freshly ground black pepper
- 4 Fermín's Flour Tortillas (page 98) or store-bought 6-inch flour tortillas
- ½ avocado, sliced, for garnish

This is a common breakfast dish served in the northern part of Mexico, where beef and flour tortillas reign supreme. Central to this dish is machaca, a finely shredded carne seca (think beef jerky floss). When not cozying up in this iconic taco, machaca can be experienced as a popular drinking snack, served with lime, hot sauce, and Maggi, the umami condiment of champions found in kitchens throughout Mexico. If you are having a particularly difficult time sourcing machaca at your neighborhood Mexican market, you'll find numerous options online to choose from (La Norteñita is a household favorite).

1. In a medium cast-iron skillet over medium heat, warm enough oil to lightly coat the bottom of the pan. Add the machaca and pico de gallo, and cook, stirring constantly, about 4 minutes. (You want to prevent the machaca from burning while incorporating the liquid of the pico de gallo.)
2. Add more oil to lightly coat the bottom of the pan and crack the eggs into the machaca mixture. Season to taste with salt and pepper, stirring constantly with a heat-resistant spatula, until the eggs are scrambled to your desired doneness.
3. On a comal, griddle, or large skillet over medium-high heat, warm the tortillas.
4. Top each tortilla with the machaca-egg mixture and garnish with the avocado and more pico de gallo.

Chicharrón in Salsa Roja Tacos

MAKES 6 TACOS

- 3 cups Salsa Roja (page 244)
- ½ cup pork or chicken stock (preferably low-sodium)
- 6 ounces store-bought fried chicharrones
- Kosher salt
- 6 Fermín's Flour Tortillas (page 98) or store-bought 6-inch flour tortillas

Garnishes

- Diced white onion
- Minced cilantro
- Salsa Verde Cruda (page 249)
- Escabeche, homemade (page 256) or store-bought

To all our line cooks out there, this simple dish has family meal written all over it. Essentially, store-bought pork rinds are cooked in salsa and served on a flour tortilla (or corn, if you please). Tacos de chicharrón are inexpensive, delicious, and just the thing to make when your favorite sous-chef forgot to order that pork shoulder you special-requested for familia. You, the seasoned professional that you are, know that "breakfast for dinner" will cause a front-of-house walkout if you so much as think of serving it again for PM fam bam. Not that you were thinking of serving French toast, combi-steamed eggs, and a coleslaw salad for fam bam—because you're better than that. [Cue the chicharrones] . . . have a good service!

1. In a medium saucepan over medium heat, warm the salsa roja and stock. Add the chicharrones and cook, stirring occasionally, until they are soft, about 20 minutes. Taste and season with salt as needed.
2. On a comal, griddle, or large skillet over medium-high heat, warm the tortillas.
3. Top each tortilla with the salsa-chicharrones mixture, the onion, and cilantro. Serve with the salsa verde cruda and escabeche on the side.

Carrot and Potato Tacos Dorados

MAKES 12 TACOS DORADOS

Potato and Carrot Mash

- 3 russet potatoes, peeled and quartered, placed in cold water to prevent browning
- 2 large carrots, cut into thirds
- Kosher salt
- 1 cup heavy cream
- ¼ cup grated Cotija cheese

Tacos Dorados

- Neutral oil
- 12 corn tortillas, homemade (page 97) or store-bought

Garnishes

- Shredded green cabbage
- Salsa Verde (page 245)
- Grated Cotija cheese
- Mexican crema
- Lime wedges

Special Equipment

- Food processor

Texture lovers, these carrot and potato tacos dorados (filled, rolled, and fried tortillas, also known as flautas or taquitos, regionally speaking, and not to be confused with the folded version of tacos dorados) are for you. We've taken inspiration from the comforting, crunchy-on-the-outside, soft-on-the-inside classic, adding carrots for a touch of sweetness. While we know from firsthand experience that it might be tempting to puree the cooked potatoes and carrots to a silky-smooth consistency, be sure to leave some chunkiness to this filling; it makes for a cleaner and more satisfying bite when it all comes together.

1. **Make the potato and carrot mash:** In a medium pot, combine the potatoes and carrots. Cover with water and salt generously. Cook over medium-high heat until the potatoes and carrots are tender, 20 to 25 minutes. Drain and set on a plate to cool slightly.
2. Meanwhile, in a small saucepan over medium-low heat, warm the cream until just simmering, about 5 minutes.
3. In a food processor, combine the softened potatoes and carrots, the warmed cream, and the cheese, then pulse until all the ingredients come together, making sure not to overmix, as this will make the potatoes gummy. Season to taste with salt and set aside.
4. **Make the tacos dorados:** In a large sauté pan over medium-low heat, warm 2 tablespoons of oil. Working with one tortilla at a time, heat the tortillas in the oil until they become pliable, about 1 minute on each side.
5. Remove the tortilla from the oil and add about 1 heaping tablespoon of the potato and carrot mash to the middle of it. Roll the tortilla into a tight cigar shape with open ends, and place seam-side down on a sheet pan. Repeat with the remaining tortillas and filling.
6. In the same pan over medium heat, add enough oil to cover the bottom of the pan. Line a plate with paper towels or set a wire rack in a sheet pan and keep near the stove.
7. Working in batches to avoid overcrowding, when the oil is hot, place the tacos dorados seam-side down in the pan and fry until golden brown and crispy, flipping halfway through, about 4 minutes total. Transfer the tacos dorados to the paper towels or rack to drain.
8. Serve the tacos dorados hot, topped with the cabbage, salsa verde, Cotija cheese, and crema, with the lime wedges on the side.

Vitamina T(ip)

Use any extra potato and carrot mash as a filling for more tacos dorados or a substitute for mashed potatoes.

Tinga Verde Tacos

MAKES 6 TACOS

- 6 corn tortillas, homemade (page 97) or store-bought, warmed
- 1½ cups Tinga Verde (recipe follows)

Garnishes

- Mexican crema
- Shredded iceberg lettuce
- Crumbled queso fresco

In these tacos, the guisado—a homey braise or stew—is served care of Masienda's very own Miguel Guerrero. One day while craving tinga, yet fresh out of tomatoes, he subbed in tomatillos, creating what has since become a family staple. Leftover tinga is also a revelation served atop tostadas.

Top each tortilla with ¼ cup of the tinga verde and garnish with the crema, shredded lettuce, and crumbled queso fresco.

Tinga Verde

This tinga gets its green color from tomatillos instead of tomatoes, but is otherwise made the same way as the classic.

MAKES 5 CUPS

- 3 boneless, skinless chicken breasts (about 1½ pounds total)
- 1 medium onion, halved
- 6 garlic cloves, peeled
- 1 bay leaf
- 1 dried chipotle chile
- 1 tablespoon Morton kosher salt, plus more as needed
- 3 tablespoons olive oil
- 10 tomatillos, husked, rinsed, and halved
- 1 serrano chile, stemmed and halved lengthwise
- 2 jalapeño chiles, stemmed and halved lengthwise
- 1 cup (loosely packed) cilantro leaves

Special Equipment

- Blender

1. In a medium pot, combine the chicken breasts, half of the onion, 2 of the garlic cloves, the bay leaf, chipotle chile, and salt. Cover with water and bring to a boil over medium-high heat. Reduce the heat to low, cover, and simmer until the chicken is cooked through and tender, 20 to 25 minutes.
2. Transfer the chicken to a bowl to cool. Strain the cooking liquid into an airtight container, discarding the solids. Measure out 1 cup of stock and set aside. (Leftover stock can be stored in the fridge for 5 to 7 days or in the freezer for 2 to 3 months.)
3. Using clean hands or 2 forks, shred the chicken as finely as possible.
4. In a medium nonstick skillet over medium heat, warm 2 tablespoons of the olive oil. Add the tomatillos, remaining 4 garlic cloves, the serrano, and the jalapeños. Sauté until softened, about 5 minutes. Remove from the heat and let cool slightly.
5. Transfer the sautéed ingredients to a blender. Add the cilantro and reserved cup of stock. Blend until the mixture reaches a uniform, pourable consistency. Season to taste with salt.
6. Slice the remaining onion half into half-moons. In the same skillet used for sautéing the ingredients, add the remaining tablespoon of olive oil and cook the onion over medium heat until softened and translucent, about 5 minutes.
7. Pour the blended sauce into the pan with the onion. Bring to a simmer and cook for another 5 minutes, allowing the flavors to meld.
8. Add the shredded chicken and stir until well combined. Cook for an additional 5 minutes, allowing the chicken to absorb the flavors of the sauce.

Carne Asada Tacos

MAKES 10 TACOS

½ bunch of cilantro, roughly chopped, stems included

½ bunch of scallions (white and green parts), roughly chopped

1 jalapeño chile, stemmed and sliced

2½ pounds flank steak

½ cup olive oil

Kosher salt and freshly ground black pepper

10 Fermín's Flour Tortillas (page 98) or store-bought 6-inch flour tortillas, warmed

Garnishes

Diced white onion

Minced cilantro

2 limes, quartered

Salsa Taquera (page 246)

Salsa de Molcajete (page 251)

Special Equipment

Blender; charcoal or gas grill or grill pan

We've all gotten bored, or perhaps curious, at some point and overdoctored a family recipe in order to make it a bit more interesting—at least us rebels and occasional troublemakers out there, anyway. This recipe in particular is a homecoming for Fermín, who worked for years on concocting the perfect asada marinade, only to one day realize that the simpler version from his childhood was never really broken, so why fix it? This asada is full-on Norteño because Fermín's a Norteño, so flour tortillas are encouraged.

1. In a blender, combine the cilantro, scallions, and jalapeño. With the blender running, slowly drizzle in the olive oil to emulsify and blend until you get a smooth paste.
2. Place the steak in a large bowl. Season the steak with salt and pepper, evenly coating its surface. Pour the mixture over the steak, turning to fully coat. Allow it to marinate in the fridge for at least 15 minutes or up to 2 hours.
3. When ready to cook the steak, remove the bowl from the fridge and bring the steak to room temperature.
4. Prepare a charcoal or gas grill for high heat. Clean the grates well and brush them with oil. (Alternatively, preheat a grill pan over medium-high heat and brush the pan with oil.) Grill the meat until you reach your desired doneness. (We like this cut medium-rare, which means grilling the steak about 3 minutes per side.) Let the steak rest for about 3 minutes, then cut against the grain into ¾-inch-thick strips, then again into ¾-inch cubes.
5. Top each tortilla with the steak, the onion, and cilantro, and serve with the lime quarters and the salsas on the side.

18+
LAGER

Smash Burger Tacos with Matchstick Fries

MAKES 4 TACOS

- 1 large russet potato
- Neutral oil, for frying
- 1 teaspoon Morton kosher salt, plus more as needed
- 1 pound ground beef (80/20 blend)
- 8 slices American cheese
- 4 Fermín's Flour Tortillas (page 98) or store-bought 6-inch flour tortillas, warmed
- 1 cup Pico de Gallo (page 253)
- ½ cup pickled jalapeños

Special Equipment

Mandoline (optional); candy/deep-fry thermometer (optional)

We've got to hand it to chef Alex Stupak for boldly highlighting this vitamina T hero dish in his *Tacos* cookbook. It is indeed an exercise in blurred lines, cultural admiration, and straight-up deliciousness that we could all stand to celebrate a bit more of—in the name of world peace. This, to be sure, is not *quite* that dish, but it is nevertheless still a big fan of world peace. At least one of the authors of this book has a full-blown addiction to smash burgers, and so it is a reflection of that dish's preparation method. This is in contrast to the classic Mexican hamburger taco, which begins as a smash burger but is then broken up and mixed in the pan with melting cheese, reading more like a chopped cheese taco.

1. Using a mandoline with the matchstick attachment, cut the potato lengthwise into thin matchsticks (⅛ × ⅛ inch). (Alternatively, using a sharp knife, thinly slice the potato lengthwise, stack the slices on top of each other in piles of 5 to 8, and slice into thin strips to create a matchstick cut.)
2. Place the matchsticks in a medium bowl and rinse under cold water for 2 to 3 minutes or until the water runs clear. Drain the matchsticks and spread them out on paper towels. Using another paper towel on top, pat them dry.
3. Pour about 2 inches of oil into a a Dutch oven or wide, heavy pot and clip a candy/deep-fry thermometer to the inside. Heat the oil over medium-high heat until the temperature reaches 350°F. (If you don't have a thermometer, dip the handle of a wooden spoon into the oil. If the oil bubbles around the handle, it's hot enough.) Line a plate with paper towels and keep near the stove.
4. Carefully place the matchsticks in the oil and fry, stirring frequently with a slotted spoon to prevent them from burning, until golden brown, 3 to 5 minutes. Using a slotted spoon, remove the fries from the oil and place on the paper towels to drain. Season to taste with salt.
5. Form the ground beef into 4 equal patties and season with the 1 teaspoon salt.
6. Set a griddle or large skillet over high heat. Cooking one at a time, add a burger patty to the griddle and use the back side of a spatula to smash it down. When the edges of the meat start to brown and the top starts to darken, flip the patty. Place 2 slices of cheese atop the patty, allow them to melt, then transfer the patty to a plate. Repeat with the remaining patties.
7. Top each tortilla with a burger patty. Garnish with the pico de gallo and matchstick potatoes, then serve with the pickled jalapeños on the side.

Tacos de Canasta

MAKES 12 TACOS

2 large potatoes (preferably russet), peeled and medium-diced, placed in a bowl of cold water to prevent browning

Kosher salt

1½ cups (12 ounces) Chorizo Rojo (page 237), uncooked

12 store-bought corn tortillas (see Tip)

1 cup thinly sliced onion (about ½ medium)

¾ cup neutral oil

1 tablespoon Aleppo pepper

1 chile de árbol

2 guajillo chiles

For Serving

Escabeche, homemade (page 256) or store-bought

Salsa de Chile de Árbol (page 250)

Salsa Verde Cruda (page 249)

Special Equipment

Large ceramic bowl or basket; candy/deep-fry thermometer (optional)

This vitamina T classic ferried via bicycles throughout Mexico City is prepared by stacking formed tacos in a canasta, or basket, and pouring hot oil over them before tucking them into butcher paper and plastic to steam. Because of this steaming effect, the dish is also known as tacos al vapor, or steamed tacos, and their texture is decidedly more moist (the good kind; don't worry) as a result. They typically appear with fillings such as chorizo and potato, like the ones we have chosen for this recipe, as well as with refried beans and chicharrón. There are other effective methods out there for re-creating this dish at home, to be sure. Some rely on the residual heat from the cooked tacos in the basket while other methods call for steaming the tacos as you would for dim sum. No matter your approach, you'll want to let them rest for about 10 minutes so that the starches in the tortilla reset and don't break on your first bite.

1. Drain the potatoes and add to a medium pot. Cover with water and salt generously. Bring to a boil over high heat. Reduce to a simmer and cook until tender, 7 to 10 minutes. Drain the potatoes.

2. In a medium sauté pan over medium-low heat, cook the chorizo, stirring constantly. When the oil starts releasing from the chorizo and the chorizo is cooked halfway so it's no longer pink, about 5 minutes, add the potatoes and stir to combine. When the chorizo is fully cooked, about 5 minutes more, remove the pan from the heat. Using a potato masher or the bottom of a cup, smash the mixture to create a chunky puree. Season to taste with salt.

3. On a comal, griddle, or large skillet over medium-high heat, warm the tortillas, then transfer to a tortilla warmer or clean kitchen towel.

4. Line a large ceramic bowl or basket with a clean kitchen towel, followed by 2 sheets of parchment paper overlapping to form an X shape, with enough overhang to wrap over the tacos once they are layered inside.

5. Fill a tortilla with about 3 tablespoons of the warm chorizo-potato mixture and fold the tortilla in half. Place it in the prepared bowl and top with a few onion slices. Repeat with the remaining ingredients, layering the tacos and onion slices in the bowl as if you were making a taco lasagna.

6. In a small saucepan over medium-high heat, heat the oil until the temperature reaches 350°F when checked with a candy/deep-fry thermometer. (If you don't have a thermometer, dip the handle of a wooden spoon into the oil. If the oil bubbles around the handle, it's hot enough.) When the oil is hot, add the Aleppo pepper and árbol and guajillo chiles and allow to bloom for 10 seconds.

7. Immediately and very carefully pour the hot oil over the tacos in the basket. Quickly fold over the parchment overhang, followed by the towel, to cover the tacos and create a warm makeshift steam oven. Allow the wrapped tacos to steam for 10 minutes.

8. Serve the tacos with the escabeche and the salsas.

Vitamina T(ip)
Avoid using homemade tortillas here, as they're more likely to fall apart when steamed.

Quesabirria

MAKES 10 TACOS

- Neutral oil
- 10 corn tortillas, homemade (page 97) or store-bought
- 1 to 2 cups Consomé (page 187), plus more for serving
- 5 cups (loosely packed) hand-pulled strands quesillo (a.k.a. queso Oaxaca), or 3¾ cups shredded low-moisture mozzarella
- 2 to 2½ cups Birria (recipe follows)

Garnishes

- Minced cilantro
- Diced white onion
- Salsa Morita (page 248), for serving
- Lime wedges, for serving

Centuries before it became internet-famous, birria, a type of slow-cooked meat served with broth, was a killer Mesoamerican method in western Mexico for spicing up wild game. A dear relative of barbacoa (see page 117), birria is believed to have originated in Jalisco. It was there that goat would eventually replace game as the birria protein of choice, following the Spanish conquest of Mexico. As it traveled north to Tijuana, the dish ultimately evolved into the social-media phenomenon that many people tend to associate with birria today: a crispy-ish taco filled with shredded braised beef that is dipped into consomé, a spicy beef broth in this case. Add melted cheese to said taco, and it becomes a quesadilla-birria taco, or quesabirria taco for short. To be sure, this is not the only or even the "original" birria—Jorge's personal favorite of all time is Birrieria Zaragoza in Chicago, FWIW—but it certainly is one version we all can't seem to get enough of.

1. Heat a lightly oiled comal, griddle, or large skillet over medium-low heat. Dip a tortilla into the fat floating on top of the consomé so that both sides are well coated, then place the tortilla on the comal and top with 2 ounces (about ½ cup) of the cheese.
2. When the cheese starts to melt, top it with ¼ cup of the birria. Fold the tortilla over itself to create a half-moon, and cook for another minute to fully melt the cheese and create a bit of a crispy crust on the outside of the tortilla. Transfer to a plate and repeat with the remaining consomé, tortillas, cheese, and birria.
3. Open each taco, add some cilantro and onion, and close.
4. Serve the tacos with the salsa and a bowl of the consomé for dipping. Serve with the lime wedges alongside to squeeze into the consomé.

RECIPE CONTINUES →

Birria and Consomé

MAKES 4 POUNDS BIRRIA AND 8 CUPS CONSOMÉ

- Kosher salt
- 8 pounds bone-in beef short ribs
- 6 cups beef stock (preferably low-sodium)
- 8 large ripe Roma (plum) tomatoes, quartered
- 1 small onion, quartered
- 4 guajillo chiles, stemmed, seeded, and veins removed
- 4 large ancho chiles, stemmed and seeded
- 4 garlic cloves, peeled
- 3 whole cloves
- 1 tablespoon black peppercorns
- 1 tablespoon allspice berries
- 1 tablespoon dried Mexican oregano
- 1 small cinnamon stick (preferably Mexican canela)
- 1 teaspoon cumin seeds

Special Equipment

Blender (preferably high-powered, such as Vitamix)

Birria and consomé keep for a while and can be eaten with tortillas or over rice, or as a filling for enchiladas or tamales.

1. Salt the outside of the short ribs to evenly cover the surface. (Don't be shy! Salt is your short ribs' friend.) Refrigerate, uncovered, for 2 hours, or preferably overnight.
2. In a medium soup pot over medium heat, combine the beef stock, tomatoes, onion, chiles, garlic, cloves, peppercorns, allspice, oregano, cinnamon stick, and cumin seeds. Cook until the vegetables and dried chiles are soft, about 25 minutes.
3. In a blender, add enough stock and solids from the pot to fill the blender no more than halfway. Blend until smooth. Repeat until all the stock and solids are blended until smooth.
4. In a large pot, combine the short ribs and blended stock. Cover and bring to a boil over medium-high heat. Reduce to a simmer and cook, covered, until the meat is tender, 2 to 3 hours.
5. Remove the short ribs from the broth and pull the meat off the bones (discard the bones). Skim the consomé to remove any large bits, then season to taste with salt. Any leftover birria and consomé can be stored in airtight containers in the fridge for 3 to 4 days.

Spicy Achiote Marinade

MAKES 2 CUPS

- 4 guajillo chiles, stemmed, seeded, and veins removed
- 2 dried puya (pulla) chiles, stemmed, seeded, and veins removed
- 1 chile de árbol, stemmed
- Finely grated zest and juice of 2 limes
- ½ medium red onion, roughly diced
- 3 garlic cloves, peeled
- 2 tablespoons apple cider vinegar
- 1 tablespoon achiote paste
- 1 teaspoon dried Mexican oregano
- ½ teaspoon ground cumin
- ½ cup olive oil
- Kosher salt

Special Equipment

Blender

This marinade is great not only for grilled fish but also for chicken, pork, or tofu. Store leftover marinade in an airtight container in the fridge for up to 10 days or in the freezer for up to 2 months.

1. In a dry skillet over medium heat, toast all of the chiles until fragrant, about 30 seconds per side. Transfer the chiles to a small bowl and cover with hot water. Let sit until softened, 15 to 20 minutes, then drain.
2. In a blender, combine the softened chiles, the lime zest and juice, onion, garlic, vinegar, achiote paste, oregano, and cumin, and blend on high until smooth, adding a little water as needed.
3. With the blender running, slowly stream in the olive oil to create an emulsified marinade. Season to taste with salt.

Pescado a la Talla

MAKES 6 TACOS

- 1 whole fish (3 to 4 pounds), such as snapper, sea bass, or grouper, butterflied, cleaned, and boned (see Tips)
- Kosher salt
- ½ cup Spicy Achiote Marinade (page 145)
- Neutral oil
- 6 corn tortillas, homemade (page 97) or store-bought, warmed
- 1 cup Charro Beans (page 239)
- Salsa Roja (page 244), for serving
- Salsa Verde Cruda (page 249), for serving
- Lime wedges, for squeezing

Special Equipment

Charcoal or gas grill (optional); large fish grilling basket (optional; see Tips)

Pescado a la talla hails from the Pacific coast of Mexico, where variations can be found from Puerto Escondido to Zihuatenejo and to Mazatlán and beyond. This dish is essentially a whole butterflied fish that is coated in an adobo and grilled. This is to say that it's less a traditional taco than a proper entrée, but because nearly everything in Mexico is consumed with tortillas, we're calling this one a taco once it's fully composed as such. You don't need a fish grilling basket to pull off pescado a la talla, but we do find it's worth the investment if you plan on making this kind of thing a regular in your dinnertime lineup. (FWIW, we're partial to the grates made by the fine folks at Made In.)

1. Pat the fish dry with paper towels. Season the whole fish with salt (don't be shy!). Generously brush the inside of the fish with the marinade, ensuring even coverage. (If using fillets, coat them on both sides.) Refrigerate the fish for at least 30 minutes, or up to 2 hours for more intense flavor.
2. While the fish is marinating, if grilling, prepare a charcoal or gas grill for high heat (or, if baking, preheat the oven to 400°F).
3. **To grill:** Brush a flat, wide fish grill basket (see Tips) with oil and place the whole fish inside, spreading it open, then close the basket. Grill over high heat, skin-side down, until crispy, 3 to 6 minutes. Flip and cook the open side of the fish for about 1 minute, until cooked through.
4. **To bake:** On a lightly oiled sheet pan, place the fish skin-side down and cook for 8 minutes. Continue to cook and check the fish every 2 minutes, until the top of the fish is white and firm to the touch.
5. Transfer the fish to a cutting board and cut into 6 pieces.
6. Assemble the tacos by topping each tortilla equally with the beans and a piece of skin-on fish. Serve with the salsas and a squeeze of lime.

Vitamina T(ips)

Ask your fishmonger to butterfly the fish if possible, or purchase 2 pounds of skin-on fillets if a whole butterflied fish is not available. If you don't have a fish grilling basket, generously spray the fish with cooking spray and very carefully place the fish on the grill, skin-side down. Do not attempt to move it until the edges of the fish start changing color and the skin begins to crisp. Using a large spatula, try to flip it (give it a little more time if it's sticking), and cook, skin-side up, until it easily releases from the grill.

TAMALES

The enduring spirit and evolution of Mexico's culinary identity

With roots dating back to the earliest of Mesoamerican times—some eight to ten thousand years ago—could there be a dish that better captures the enduring spirit and evolution of Mexico's culinary identity than the tamal? Tamales are the stuff of legends, perhaps the earliest dish to be made from nixtamalized corn (field corn cooked and soaked in highly alkaline water)—like, ever. They are Bonnie to Mexico's Clyde, the Jay to its Bey; a ride-or-die union that went on the run, touring across much of the world, ultimately influencing nearly all of Latin America, North America, and even parts of Asia with their sensational, steamy selves.

"What is a tamal?" you ask? Tamales are masa (corn dough) cakes, often handheld in size, that may be stuffed with vegetables, meats, cheeses, and/or herbs. They owe their form to their unique wrapping, which in Mexico commonly includes corn husks or banana leaves; without it, they'd be nothing but unformed corn dough, which, incidentally, is what tamal, or tamalli, means in Nahuatl.

For as long as they've been a thing, tamales have been a celebratory food. In ancient Mesoamerican times, they were both offered up and thrown down during important religious ceremonies. They have also, however, been an exceptional food to be consumed on the go for taking on journeys, accompanying early Mesoamericans as they traveled by land. Given their self-contained and portable nature, perhaps it's no wonder they continue to define Mexico's storied street-food landscape to this very day.

The dough (masa) for tamales is not the same as the masa for tortillas—the texture and even the ingredients are different. Tamal masa almost always involves some combination of ground nixtamalized corn, whipped fat (lard is most common, but you can use coconut oil, vegan shortening, or even butter), broth, and salt. While you can often buy prepared masa at a tortillería or supermercado, making it at home from masa harina is simple and satisfying.

TAMAL TIPS

Mix Master

To achieve a fluffy texture in your finished tamales, you'll want to introduce as much air into the dough as possible by whipping the fat until it looks almost like cake frosting. If you don't have a stand mixer, use an electric hand mixer (though you may need to work in batches for similar results). The goal is a wet, spreadable dough.

Work Smarter, Not Harder

Tamales are a labor of love, typically meant as a full-day (even two-day) project, with extra hands welcome. To speed things up, you can make the masa and the fillings up to 3 days in advance.

Just Like Snowflakes

Corn husks and banana leaves vary widely in size. While each tamal recipe specifies a quantity of filling, use your best judgment to adjust the quantity of masa and filling based on the size of your husk or leaf.

More Is More

We always call for extra corn husks or banana leaves in tamales recipes to account for any that are torn or too-big/too-small. Use any leftovers to line the bottom of your steamer basket to prevent burning!

The Penny Trick

To avoid a scorched steamer and burnt tamales, place a clean coin in the bottom of your tamalera or pot. When steaming, if you hear the coin rattle, you'll know it's time to add more water.

Money in the Bank

If you're making a big batch of tamales, save some for a rainy day! Cooked tamales can be refrigerated for 1 to 2 days, or frozen for up to 6 months. Allow them to cool after steaming, then store in an airtight container or freezer bag.

Tamales Like It Hot

To reheat tamales, steam them on the stovetop for 20 to 30 minutes, or wrap each tamal in a damp paper towel and microwave for 2 to 5 minutes. Alternatively, heat them on a hot comal in their husks—the deeper the char, the better the flavor. To take it to the next level, remove the tamal from the husk and pan-fry in a bit of oil until crispy on either side.

Duck in Mole Negro Tamales (page 169)

Rajas con Queso Tamales

MAKES 20 TO 24 TAMALES

Rajas Filling

- 8 poblano chiles
- 4 fresh Hatch chiles, or any spicy green chile, such as jalapeño or serrano
- Neutral oil
- Kosher salt
- 2 medium onions, sliced
- 6 cups fresh corn kernels (from about 8 ears)
- 2 cups heavy cream

Tamales

- 4 cups (480g; loosely packed) masa harina, plus more as needed
- ½ cup (110g) refined coconut oil
- 1 tablespoon Morton kosher salt, plus more as needed
- 5 cups (1200g) vegetable stock, plus more as needed (preferably low-sodium)
- 20 to 30 dried corn husks
- 5 cups (loosely packed) hand-pulled strands quesillo (a.k.a. queso Oaxaca), or 3¾ cups shredded low-moisture mozzarella

Special Equipment

Stand mixer or electric hand mixer; tamalera (tamal steamer) or large pot with steamer basket/insert

Rajas are nearly as ubiquitous in Mexican cooking as tamales themselves. While they colloquially refer to any kind of "strips" made from chiles, they are invariably made from chiles poblanos. Once the chiles are roasted, seeded, and cut into strips, the rajas can be assembled into salads, garnishes, taco fillings, and beyond. While not strictly "traditional," Hatch chiles are added here for a touch of warmth. Jalapeños or serranos will also char nicely while adding a moderate dose of spice to each bite.

1 **Make the rajas filling:** In a medium bowl, toss the poblano and Hatch chiles with a light amount of neutral oil and salt. Over an open flame, char the chiles until their skins turn black all over, rotating as needed. (Alternatively, use the oven. Roast for 10 minutes at 450°F, then flip and roast for another 10 minutes or until fully blistered.) Transfer the chiles to the bowl and cover with a plate or a kitchen towel to allow them to steam for 10 minutes, then let cool.

2 When the chiles have cooled, remove their stem ends and peel off the charred skins. Halve the chiles lengthwise, then remove as many seeds as possible. Cut into ¼-inch-wide strips (rajas) and set aside.

3 In a medium pot over medium heat, heat 2 tablespoons of neutral oil. Add the onions and cook, stirring constantly, until translucent, 3 to 4 minutes. Add the corn and continue to cook, until the corn brightens in color and softens in texture, 5 more minutes. Add the rajas and the cream. Cook until the cream is reduced by two-thirds, about 15 minutes depending on how wide the pot is. Taste and season with salt as needed. Set aside.

4 **Make the masa:** In a stand mixer fitted with the paddle attachment, combine the masa harina, coconut oil, and salt. Whip on medium speed (setting 5 or 6 on a KitchenAid) until it is a smooth, homogeneous texture. With the mixer on low speed (setting 2), slowly stream in the vegetable stock until it all comes together. (Alternatively, combine the ingredients in small batches using an electric hand mixer on low speed.) The masa should feel well hydrated (not gritty) with a creamy, airy texture that's easy to spread (think hummus or cake batter). If it's too dry, add more stock; if it's too wet, add more masa harina, whipping to incorporate. Taste and season with salt as needed. Set aside.

5 In a large bowl, combine the corn husks and enough hot water to cover. Soak the husks until soft, about 20 minutes. Gently wring out the husks and pat them dry with a kitchen towel.

How to Fill & Fold Tamales (Corn Husk)

6 **Assemble the tamales:** Working with one corn husk at a time, lay it on a work surface with the smooth side facing up and the wide end closest to you. Using a spoon, spatula, or bench scraper, spread a thin, even layer of masa (about ⅓ cup, depending on the size of the husk) from side to side, leaving the narrow end uncovered; you're looking to cover an area about 3 × 5 inches. Add ¼ cup of the rajas and ¼ cup of the cheese to the center of the masa. Fold the left side of the husk over the filling to cover it, then fold the right side so it overlaps the other side of the husk. Fold the pointy top down toward the bottom (wide) side of the husk, about halfway. Place the tamal on a plate or sheet pan, folded-side down. Repeat with the remaining husks, masa, and cheese. Never done this before? Scan the QR code to see how.

7 **Steam the tamales:** Fill the bottom of a tamalera or a pot with a steamer basket/insert with water. Place the tamales upright in the basket, with the open ends facing up. Cover and steam over medium-high heat for 55 minutes. Check for doneness by trying to pull the husk from a tamal; if it pulls away from the masa easily then they're ready!

8 Remove the pot from the heat and let the tamales rest, covered, for about 15 minutes. The tamales will firm up as they cool.

9 To serve, open the tamales and enjoy warm.

Pork Tamales with Chile Colorado

MAKES 20 TO 24 TAMALES

Pork Filling

- 2 cups pork or chicken stock, plus more as needed (preferably low-sodium)
- 3 guajillo chiles, stemmed, seeded, and veins removed
- 15 chiles de árbol
- 1 tablespoon piquín chiles
- 2 ripe Roma (plum) tomatoes, quartered
- 1 medium onion, roughly diced
- ½ cup distilled white vinegar
- 6 garlic cloves, peeled
- 2 tablespoons annatto seeds
- 10 fresh epazote leaves, or 5 dried epazote sprigs
- 1 dried avocado leaf
- 1 bay leaf
- Kosher salt
- 2½ pounds boneless pork shoulder, cut into 3-inch chunks
- Neutral oil

So comforting and delicious are these pork tamales, it's no small wonder some riff on this combination can be found throughout much of Mexico, Central America, and the United States. We use annatto here, and though it isn't commonly added, it makes for a beautiful color and citrusy note that we quite like. This particular variation on the theme is for those who like it hot. While the called-for fifteen chiles de árbol and a tablespoon of chile piquín might read as especially extreme, rest assured there's just enough acidity and porky richness to balance the Scovilles. And if you're still looking for just a touch more heat, consider a last dab or two of Salsa de Chile de Árbol (page 250) to finish.

1. **Make the pork filling:** In a large saucepan over medium-high heat, bring the stock to a simmer.
2. Meanwhile, place the guajillo chiles, chiles de árbol, and piquín chiles in a large heatproof bowl. When the stock is hot, pour it over the chiles and allow them to soften for 8 to 10 minutes.
3. Drain the chiles and transfer to a blender, reserving their soaking liquid. Add the tomatoes, onion, vinegar, garlic, annatto seeds, epazote, avocado leaf, and bay leaf, and turn the machine on. Slowly stream in all the reserved chile-soaking liquid to make a smooth puree. This will serve as the braising liquid base for the pork.
4. Salt the pork, lightly covering every side. Set a Dutch oven or wide, heavy pot over medium-high heat and add enough oil to cover the bottom of the pot. Working in batches to avoid overcrowding, when the oil is hot, sear the pork chunks on all sides until browned, turning as needed, 2 to 3 minutes per side.
5. Return all the pork to the Dutch oven and carefully pour in the braising liquid base. Bring to a boil over medium-high heat, then reduce the heat to medium and simmer, covered, until the pork is tender, 2½ to 3 hours. Taste and season with salt as needed then let the pork cool in its cooking liquid.
6. Remove the pork from the pot and reserve the braising liquid. Using 2 forks or your hands, shred the pork and set it aside. Measure out 5 cups (1200g) of the pork-braising liquid (if you have less than 5 cups, supplement with chicken stock).

Tamales

½ cup (100g) lard

4 cups (480g; loosely packed) masa harina, plus more as needed

1 tablespoon Morton kosher salt, plus more as needed

20 to 30 dried corn husks

Special Equipment

Blender; digital scale; stand mixer or electric hand mixer; tamalera (tamal steamer) or large pot with steamer basket/insert

How to Fill & Fold Tamales (Corn Husk)

7 **Make the masa:** In a stand mixer fitted with the paddle attachment, whip the lard on high speed (setting 10 on a KitchenAid) until light and fluffy. With the mixer on low speed (setting 2), add the masa harina and salt. Slowly stream in 4 to 5 cups of the pork-braising liquid and allow the mixture to come together. (Alternatively, combine the ingredients in small batches using an electric hand mixer on low speed.) The masa should feel well hydrated (not gritty) with a creamy, airy texture that's easy to spread (think hummus or cake batter). If it's too dry, add more liquid; if it's too wet, add more masa harina, whipping to incorporate. Taste and season with salt as needed. Set aside.

8 In a large bowl, combine the corn husks and enough hot water to cover. Soak the husks until soft, about 20 minutes. Gently wring out the husks and pat them dry with a kitchen towel.

9 **Assemble the tamales:** Working with one corn husk at a time, lay it on a work surface with the smooth side facing up and the wide end closest to you. Using a spoon, spatula, or bench scraper, spread a thin, even layer of masa (about ⅓ cup, depending on the size of the husk) from side to side, leaving the narrow end uncovered; you're looking to cover an area about 3 × 5 inches. Add ¼ cup of the shredded pork to the center of the masa. Fold the left side of the husk over the filling to cover it, then fold the right side so it overlaps the other side of the husk. Fold the pointy top down toward the bottom (wide) side of the husk, about halfway. Place on a plate or sheet pan, folded-side down. Repeat with the remaining husks, masa, and pork. Never done this before? Scan the QR code to see how.

10 **Steam the tamales:** Fill the bottom of a tamalera or a pot with steamer basket/insert with water. Place the tamales upright in the basket, with the open ends facing up. Cover and steam over medium-high heat for 55 minutes. Check for doneness by trying to pull the husk from a tamal; if it pulls away from the masa easily then they're ready!

11 Remove the pot from the heat and let the tamales rest, covered, for about 15 minutes. The tamales will firm up as they cool.

12 To serve, open the tamales and enjoy warm.

Bean and Cheese Tamales

MAKES 20 TO 24 TAMALES

- 6 tablespoons (80g) refined coconut oil
- 2 cups (520g) Smoky Refried Beans (page 238, made with black beans), plus more for serving
- 3 cups (360g; loosely packed) masa harina, plus more as needed
- 1 tablespoon Morton kosher salt, plus more as needed
- 1 cup (240g) Roasted Vegetable Stock (page 161) or store-bought stock, plus more as needed
- 20 to 30 banana leaves, tough middle ribs removed, cut into 9 × 12-inch rectangles
- 4 cups (loosely packed) hand-pulled strands quesillo (a.k.a. queso Oaxaca), or 3 cups shredded low-moisture mozzarella
- ½ cup grated Cotija cheese (optional), for serving

Special Equipment

Stand mixer or electric hand mixer; tamalera (tamal steamer) or large pot with steamer basket/insert

How to Fill & Fold Tamales (Banana Leaf)

Simple these tamales are; however, basic they are not. While this combination of ingredients is used throughout Mexico, those hailing from towns along the border (like, say, one of this cookbook's authors) might be inclined to claim the bean and cheese tamal as their region's very own creation. In a bit of a twist, here, chipotle-infused beans are refried and folded into the tamal masa itself, making for an ethereal, leguminous bite.

1. **Make the masa:** In a stand mixer fitted with the paddle attachment, combine the coconut oil and refried black beans, and whip on medium-low speed (setting 4 on a KitchenAid) until smooth. With the mixer still running, slowly add the masa harina in 3 batches, followed by the salt, until a uniform dough forms. With the mixer on low speed (setting 2), stream in the vegetable stock to create a homogeneous tamal dough, 3 to 5 minutes. (Alternatively, combine the ingredients in small batches using an electric hand mixer on low speed.) The masa should feel well hydrated (not gritty) with a smooth, almost pourable texture (think sour cream). If it's too dry, add more stock; if it's too wet, add more masa harina, whipping to incorporate. Taste and season with salt as needed. Set aside.
2. **Assemble the tamales:** Heat a comal, griddle, or large skillet over medium-high heat and warm the banana leaves on both sides, 15 to 20 seconds per side, or until they turn a deep green color and become fragrant. Don't skip this step; it will make them pliable and prevent cracking or breaking.
3. Fill the middle of each banana leaf with about ½ cup of the prepared masa (depending on the size of the leaf), then sprinkle a generous amount of quesillo on top. Fold the top and bottom sides of the leaf over the masa, then fold over the sides so that it looks like a rectangular present. Place seam-side down on a sheet pan or plate. Repeat with the remaining ingredients. Never done this before? Scan the QR code to see how.
4. **Steam the tamales:** Fill the bottom of a tamalera or a pot with steamer basket/insert with water. Place your tamales flat in the basket, staggering them on top of each other evenly in the pot. Cover and steam over medium-high heat for 45 minutes. Check for doneness by trying to pull the husk from a tamal; if it pulls away from the masa easily then they're ready!
5. Remove the pot from the heat and let the tamales rest, covered, for about 15 minutes. The tamales will firm up as they cool.
6. To serve, open the tamales and cover them with more of the refried black beans and the grated Cotija, if desired.

RECIPE CONTINUES →

YOGURT
con Fruta

Roasted Vegetable Stock

MAKES ABOUT 2 CUPS

- 1 medium butternut squash, peeled, seeded, and cut into large cubes
- 2 medium onions, roughly chopped
- 2 cups roughly chopped celery (about 5 stalks)
- 2 cups roughly chopped unpeeled carrots (about 4 medium)
- 2 tablespoons olive oil
- 2 teaspoons Morton kosher salt
- 2 bay leaves

When it comes to vegetable stock, you can opt for store-bought, of course, but roasted butternut squash is this stock's secret to a hint of sweetness and extra-silky texture. Use as a base for soups or stews, or in the masa for any vegetarian tamales, such as Rajas con Queso Tamales (page 154) or Achiote Mushroom Tamales (page 166).

1 Preheat the oven to 350°F.

2 In a medium bowl, combine the squash, onions, celery, and carrots with the olive oil and salt, then toss to coat. Spread on a sheet pan and roast until the vegetables soften slightly, 20 minutes.

3 Transfer the roasted vegetables to a stock pot or Dutch oven. Add the bay leaves and 2 quarts of water, and bring to a boil over medium-high heat. Reduce the heat and simmer until the stock deepens in color and smells sweeter and more aromatic, about 2 hours. Strain and discard the vegetables. Store the stock in an airtight container in the fridge for up to 1 week or in the freezer for up to 3 months.

Chicken in Mole Verde Tamales

MAKES 20 TO 24 TAMALES

1 whole chicken (3 to 4 pounds)

2½ tablespoons Morton kosher salt, plus more as needed

Mole Verde (recipe follows)

½ cup (100g) lard

4 cups (480g; loosely packed) masa harina, plus more as needed

5 cups (1200g) chicken stock, plus more as needed (preferably low-sodium)

20 to 30 dried corn husks

Special Equipment

Stand mixer or electric hand mixer; tamalera (tamal steamer) or large pot with steamer basket/insert

For masters of the mole, feel free to get straight to cooking. For the mole uninitiated, a pop quiz . . .

True or false:
(1) All moles have chocolate.
(2) All moles require painstaking preparation.

False on both counts! As far as moles go, mole verde—an herby, pepita-based sauce (slash) stew—is perhaps the easiest and most time-efficient style of mole to prepare at home. Regional variations on this dish abound throughout Mexico, offering a range of proteins and herb blends to choose from, but you can count on this recipe leaning lighter and brighter on the flavor spectrum.

1. Preheat the oven to 400°F. Line a sheet pan with parchment paper.
2. Using a sharp knife or kitchen shears, remove the chicken's backbone and lay the chicken flat on the sheet pan, making sure to press down on the breast bone so it cracks and flattens completely. Pat the chicken dry with paper towels and sprinkle with 1½ tablespoons of the salt.
3. Roast for 50 minutes, until the skin is golden brown and clear juices run out of the breast when poked with a sharp knife, then remove from the oven, and let rest for 10 minutes. When the chicken is cool enough to handle, remove the meat from the bones and shred it into a large bowl.
4. In a medium saucepan over medium heat, combine the mole verde and the shredded chicken. Stir until all the ingredients are combined and the chicken is warmed through, about 15 minutes. Season to taste with salt and set aside.
5. **Make the masa:** In a stand mixer fitted with the paddle attachment, whip the lard on high speed (setting 10 on a KitchenAid) until light and fluffy. With the mixer on low speed (setting 2), add the masa harina and salt. Slowly stream in the chicken stock until it all comes together. (Alternatively, combine the ingredients in small batches using an electric hand mixer on low speed.) The masa should feel well hydrated (not gritty) with a creamy, airy texture that's easy to spread (think hummus or cake batter). If it's too dry, add more stock; if it's too wet, add more masa harina, whipping to incorporate. Taste and season with salt as needed. Set aside.
6. In a large bowl, combine the corn husks and enough hot water to cover. Soak the husks until soft, about 20 minutes. Gently wring out the husks and pat them dry with a kitchen towel.

How to Fill & Fold Tamales (Corn Husk)

7 **Assemble the tamales:** Working with one corn husk at a time, lay it on a work surface with the smooth side facing up and the wide end closest to you. Using a spoon, spatula, or bench scraper, spread a thin, even layer of masa (about ⅓ cup, depending on the size of the husk) from side to side, leaving the narrow end uncovered; you're looking to cover an area about 3 × 5 inches. Add ¼ cup of the chicken mixture to the center of the masa. Fold the left side of the husk over the filling to cover it, then fold the right side so it overlaps the other side of the husk. Fold the pointy top down toward the bottom (wide) side of the husk, about halfway. Place on a plate or sheet pan, folded-side down. Repeat with the remaining husks, masa, and chicken. Never done this before? Scan the QR code to see how.

8 **Steam the tamales:** Fill the bottom of a tamalera or a pot with steamer basket/insert with water. Place the tamales upright in the basket, with the open ends facing up. Cover and steam over medium-high heat for 55 minutes. Check for doneness by trying to pull the husk from a tamal; if it pulls away from the masa easily then they're ready!

9 Remove the pot from the heat and let the tamales rest, covered, for about 15 minutes. The tamales will firm up as they cool.

10 To serve, open the tamales and enjoy warm.

RECIPE CONTINUES →

Mole Verde

What makes this mole a breeze to prep is the absence of dried chiles, as found in a classic mole negro (see page 171). If, however, you're still pining for more prep, you may consider blanching the herbs ahead of time, which will lend the mole a more vibrant green color. Though recipes will vary by region and household, a healthy base of pepitas is a constant.

Nota buena:
Mole verde is sometimes also called pipián; however, it's important to note that not all pipiáns are technically green—there are white and red examples, as well.

MAKES 5½ CUPS

- 1¼ cups raw pumpkin seeds
- Neutral oil
- 10 ripe tomatillos, husked, rinsed, and quartered
- 1 bunch of scallions (white and green parts), sliced
- 10 garlic cloves, peeled
- 2 allspice berries
- 2 whole cloves
- 1 tablespoon cumin seeds
- 1½ teaspoons coriander seeds
- 3 cups chicken stock (preferably low-sodium)
- 1 head of romaine lettuce
- 1 bunch of parsley
- 1 bunch of cilantro
- ¼ cup fresh mint leaves
- ¼ cup fresh epazote leaves (optional)
- Kosher salt

Special Equipment

Blender

1. Preheat the oven to 350°F.
2. Place the pumpkin seeds on a sheet pan and toast, tossing every few minutes, until they become golden, about 10 minutes. Be careful not to let them burn. Set aside.
3. In a medium saucepan over medium heat, add enough oil to cover the bottom of the pan. Add the tomatillos, scallions, and garlic and cook for 8 minutes, stirring occasionally. Once the tomatillos have softened, add the allspice, cloves, cumin seeds, and coriander seeds and cook, stirring constantly, until the spices become fragrant, about 2 minutes. Add the chicken stock and the toasted pumpkin seeds, then bring to a simmer and cook over low heat to bring the flavors together, about 20 minutes. Remove the pot from the heat and let cool slightly.
4. Working in batches, add the tomatillo mixture to a blender and blend until smooth. Again in batches, transfer the puree back to the same saucepan.
5. Roughly chop the romaine, parsley, cilantro, mint, and epazote (if using). Add all the greens to the blender and blend on high until a smooth puree forms. Add the puree to the saucepan and stir to combine. Bring to a simmer over medium heat and cook for 5 minutes, stirring occasionally. Season to taste with salt. Store the mole in an airtight container in the fridge for 3 to 5 days or in the freezer for about 1 month.

PRIORIDAD
DE USO

Achiote Mushroom Tamales

MAKES 14 TO 20 TAMALES

Achiote Base

- 1 onion, quartered
- 10 garlic cloves, peeled
- 1 cup annatto seeds (about 5 ounces)
- 2 tablespoons dried Mexican oregano
- 1 tablespoon cumin seeds
- 2 allspice berries
- 2 whole cloves
- 1 cinnamon stick (preferably Mexican canela)
- 1 bay leaf
- 1 cup fresh orange juice (about 3 oranges)
- ½ cup fresh lime juice (about 3 limes)
- ½ cup fresh grapefruit juice (about 1 grapefruit)
- ½ cup olive oil

Mushroom Filling

- 2½ pounds fresh lion's mane or oyster mushrooms
- 2 tablespoons olive oil
- Kosher salt

This one's a loose, veggie-forward take on cochinita pibil, the slow-roasted, barbecue-esque pork and achiote dish from Mexico's Yucatán Peninsula. This recipe is technically vegetarian, but not in the jackfruit-trying-to-be-shredded-meat kind of way. (No judgment if you're into jackfruit, BTW.) Anyway, thanks to the proliferation of at-home grow kits and vertical farm start-ups across the United States, it has never been easier to get your hands on lion's mane mushrooms. If, however, you are unable to find this variety locally, shredded oyster mushrooms will still bring the magic.

1. **Make the achiote base:** In a blender, combine the onion, garlic, annatto seeds, oregano, cumin seeds, allspice berries, cloves, cinnamon stick, bay leaf, orange juice, lime juice, grapefruit juice, and olive oil, and blend until smooth. Set 2 cups of the puree aside for the masa preparation and reserve the rest for use in the filling.
2. **Make the mushroom filling:** Use clean hands to shred the mushrooms by hand into strands (as with pulled pork, see page 156).
3. In a medium saucepan over medium heat, warm the olive oil. Add the mushrooms and sauté until slightly softened, 5 to 6 minutes. Add the reserved achiote base, reduce the heat to medium-low, and cook the mushrooms, stirring occasionally, for 20 minutes to allow all the flavors to come together. Season to taste with salt. (It is important to wait to add salt until the end of the cooking process to avoid mushy mushrooms.)

Tamales

3 cups (360g; loosely packed) masa harina, plus more as needed

1 tablespoon Morton kosher salt, plus more as needed

2 cups (480g) vegetable stock, plus more as needed (preferably low-sodium)

½ cup (110g) olive oil

14 to 20 banana leaves, tough middle ribs removed, cut into 9 × 12-inch rectangles

2 cups (loosely packed) hand-pulled strands quesillo (a.k.a. queso Oaxaca), or 1½ cups shredded low-moisture mozzarella

Habanero-Pickled Onions (page 257), for serving

Special Equipment

Blender (preferably high-powered, such as Vitamix); stand mixer or electric hand mixer; tamalera (tamal steamer) or large pot with steamer basket/insert

How to Fill & Fold Tamales (Banana Leaf)

4 **Make the masa:** In a stand mixer fitted with the paddle attachment, combine the masa harina, salt, vegetable stock, and the reserved 2 cups achiote base, and beat on medium speed (setting 5 or 6 on a KitchenAid) until it comes together. With the mixer on low speed (setting 2), slowly stream in the olive oil until it's fully incorporated but slightly loose. (Alternatively, combine the ingredients in small batches using an electric hand mixer on low speed.) The masa should feel well hydrated (not gritty) with a smooth, almost pourable texture (think sour cream). If it's too dry, add more oil; if it's too wet, add more masa harina, whipping to incorporate. Taste and season with salt as needed. Set aside.

5 **Assemble the tamales:** Heat a comal, griddle, or large skillet over medium-high heat and warm the banana leaves on both sides, 15 to 20 seconds per side, or until they turn a deep green color and become fragrant. Don't skip this step; it will make them pliable and prevent cracking or breaking.

6 Fill the middle of each banana leaf with about ½ cup of the prepared masa (depending on the size of the leaf), followed by 2 heaping tablespoons of the mushroom filling. Top with a generous sprinkle of the quesillo. Fold the top and bottom sides of the leaf over the masa, then fold over the sides so that it looks like a rectangular present. Place seam-side down on a sheet pan or plate. Repeat with the remaining ingredients. Never done this before? Scan the QR code to see how.

7 **Steam the tamales:** Fill the bottom of a tamalera or a pot with steamer basket/insert with water. Place the tamales flat in the basket, staggering them on top of each other evenly in the pot. Cover and steam over medium-high heat for 45 minutes. Check for doneness by trying to pull the husk from a tamal; if it pulls away from the masa easily then they're ready!

8 Remove the pot from the heat and let the tamales rest, covered, for about 15 minutes. The tamales will firm up as they cool.

9 Open the tamales and serve with habanero-pickled onions.

Duck in Mole Negro Tamales

MAKES 20 TO 24 TAMALES

Duck Confit

- 6 duck legs
- Kosher salt
- 7 to 10 cups duck fat, neutral oil, or lard

Duck Filling

- 2½ cups Mole Negro (recipe follows)
- 2 cups chicken stock (preferably low-sodium)

Tamales

- 4 cups (480g; loosely packed) masa harina, plus more as needed
- 1 tablespoon Morton kosher salt, plus more as needed
- 5 cups (1200g) chicken stock, plus more as needed (preferably low-sodium)
- 20 to 30 dried corn husks

Special Equipment

Stand mixer or electric hand mixer; tamalera (tamal steamer) or large pot with steamer basket/insert

Look, friends, I [Jorge, here] am not going to sugarcoat it: This dish is a beast. I feel about attempting mole negro the way I do about preparing a hundred-layer lasagna, laminated pastries, or Edomae sushi at home: It's a dish I soulfully savor but personally leave to the experts. If I'm craving it back home in LA, I'll either cheat with a premade mole paste and some chicken broth or skip the cooking altogether and go straight to my neighborhood Oaxacan restaurant for a heaping slice of humble pie. I'm just not worthy.

And as if mole negro were not a high-enough art form on its own, this recipe had to kick things up another notch with the duck confit and the tamal assembly, to boot. There's climbing Everest, and then there's climbing Everest without oxygen in the month of January. But then again, some of you are fearless and talented enough to do it (like my co-author, Fermín), so namaste to y'all.

1. **Make the duck confit:** Place the duck legs flat on a sheet pan or baking dish that fits in your fridge. Salt the duck legs enough to lightly cover all the surfaces. Refrigerate, uncovered, for at least 6 hours or preferably overnight.
2. Preheat the oven to 250°F.
3. Run the duck legs under cold water to rinse off as much salt as possible. Pat them dry and place them in a baking pan or Dutch oven large enough to fit them and the 7 to 10 cups of fat.
4. In a medium saucepan, melt the duck fat over medium heat until it's just liquid. Pour as much fat as is needed to submerge the duck legs completely in the baking pan. Transfer the pan to the oven and cook, covered, until the meat pulls easily off the bone, about 4½ hours.
5. Remove the duck from the oven and allow it to cool slightly. Transfer the duck legs (without the fat) to a wire rack set over a sheet pan. Let the legs drain for 5 minutes, then remove the meat from the bones and use clean hands or 2 forks to shred it into a medium bowl. The duck skin can be finely chopped and mixed in with the duck meat. (Alternatively, heat up some of the reserved duck fat and fry the skin until crispy, then chop it and mix with the rest of the duck.)
6. When the duck fat is completely cooled but not yet solid, strain it. Measure ½ cup of the fat and set it aside for the masa preparation. (Store any remaining duck fat in an airtight container in the fridge for up to 1 month. Use it to roast vegetables, fry potatoes, or spread on tostadas.)

RECIPE CONTINUES →

How to Fill & Fold Tamales (Corn Husk)

7 **Make the duck filling:** In a medium saucepan, combine the mole negro and the chicken stock. Heat it over medium-low until the sauce comes to a light simmer, about 6 minutes. Add the chopped duck and cook until warmed through, about 5 minutes. Set aside.

8 **Make the masa:** In a stand mixer fitted with the paddle attachment, combine the masa harina, the reserved ½ cup duck fat, and the salt. Whip on medium speed (setting 5 or 6 on a KitchenAid) until it comes together. With the mixer on low speed (setting 2), slowly stream in the chicken stock, whipping until it is smooth and comes together. (Alternatively, combine the ingredients in small batches using an electric hand mixer on low speed.) The masa should feel well hydrated (not gritty) with a creamy, airy texture that's easy to spread (think hummus or cake batter). If it's too dry, add more stock; if it's too wet, add more masa harina, whipping to incorporate. Taste and season with more salt as needed. Set aside.

9 In a large bowl, combine the corn husks and enough hot water to cover. Soak the husks in hot water until soft, about 20 minutes. Gently wring out the husks and pat them dry with a kitchen towel.

10 **Assemble the tamales:** Working with one corn husk at a time, lay it on a work surface with the smooth side facing up and the wide end closest to you. Using a spoon, spatula, or bench scraper, spread a thin, even layer of masa (about ⅓ cup, depending on the size of the husk) from side to side, leaving the narrow end uncovered; you're looking to cover an area about 3 × 5 inches. Add ¼ cup of the duck in mole negro to the center of the masa. Fold the left side of the husk over the filling to cover it, then fold the right side so it overlaps the other side of the husk. Fold the pointy top down toward the bottom (wide) side of the husk, about halfway. Place on a plate or sheet pan, folded-side down. Repeat with the remaining husks, masa, and duck. Never done this before? Scan the QR code to see how.

11 **Steam the tamales:** Fill the bottom of a tamalera or a pot with steamer basket/insert with water. Place the tamales upright in the basket, with the open ends facing up. Cover and steam over medium-high heat for 55 minutes. Check for doneness by trying to pull the husk from a tamal; if it pulls away from the masa easily then they're ready!

12 Remove the pot from the heat and let the tamales rest, covered, for about 15 minutes. The tamales will firm up as they cool.

13 To serve, open the tamales and enjoy warm.

RECIPE CONTINUES →

Mole Negro

MAKES 4 CUPS

- 15 pasilla chiles, stemmed, seeded, and veins removed
- 15 mulato or ancho chiles, stemmed and seeded
- Neutral oil
- 1 cup raw peanuts
- 1 cup raw almonds (preferably slivered)
- 1 cup raw pecans
- 1 cup garlic cloves, peeled
- ½ cup sliced peeled fresh ginger
- 4 dried avocado leaves
- 1 bunch of thyme (about ½ ounce)
- ½ cup sesame seeds
- 2 cinnamon sticks (preferably Mexican canela)
- 1 tablespoon anise seeds
- 1 tablespoon allspice berries
- 2 medium onions, roughly diced
- 1 cup prunes
- 1 cup raisins
- 1 cup tomato paste
- 10 ounces high-quality 85% dark chocolate (such as La Rifa or Taza), roughly chopped

Special Equipment

Blender (preferably high-powered, such as Vitamix)

As long as you're committed to making this labor-intensive mole, you should prepare enough to make the effort worth it. You can store it in an airtight container in the fridge for 7 to 10 days or up to 6 months in the freezer. When ready to use, heat the paste with as much stock of your choice as is needed to reach your desired consistency.

1. Preheat the oven to 400°F.
2. Place the pasilla and mulato chiles in a single layer on a sheet pan and bake until blackened, 12 to 15 minutes. Transfer the chiles to a large bowl and set aside. (This bowl will hold all the mole ingredients, so make sure to use the largest you have.)
3. In a large sauté pan over medium heat, heat 1½ tablespoons of oil. Add the peanuts and toast until golden brown, about 5 minutes; add to the bowl with the chiles. Repeat this with the almonds and then the pecans, adding more oil to the pan as necessary to evenly coat the nuts as they cook.
4. Wipe out the pan, add 1½ tablespoons of oil, and warm over medium heat. Add the garlic and ginger and fry until golden, about 6 minutes. Add the avocado leaves, thyme, sesame seeds, cinnamon, anise seeds, and allspice berries and cook, stirring, until fragrant, about 3 minutes. Remove from the heat and add this mixture to the bowl with the chiles and nuts.
5. Wipe out the pan again, add enough oil to cover the bottom, and warm over medium heat. Add the onions and fry until golden brown, about 5 minutes. Transfer the onions to the large bowl.
6. Add the prunes to the pan and cook until soft, 3 to 4 minutes. Transfer to the large bowl. Repeat this step with the raisins. Mix the ingredients in the large bowl until combined.
7. Working in small batches, add some of the bowl's ingredients to a blender with just enough water to get things moving, and blend on high until a thick paste forms. Repeat until all the ingredients are blended into a paste.
8. Set a Dutch oven or large, heavy pot over medium heat and add enough oil to cover the bottom of the pot. Fry the tomato paste, stirring constantly to prevent it from burning, until it changes color from bright to dark red, about 10 minutes.
9. Add the mole paste to the tomato paste, and use a wooden spoon to stir until combined. Turn the heat to low and cook for 4 hours, stirring occasionally.
10. After 4 hours, add the chocolate and cook for 1 more hour over low heat, stirring occasionally. (This long cooking process draws out any remaining moisture from the paste, deepening its flavor as the sugars caramelize; it also allows it to be stored for longer.)
11. Allow the paste to cool completely before storing in an airtight container in the fridge or freezer.

55 9187 5565
55 3404 8871
4creativo
55 9130 7374
55 8926 2855
HSBC
HSBC

Short Rib Tamales

MAKES 20 TO 24 TAMALES

Beef Filling

- 5 pounds bone-in beef short ribs
- ¼ cup dried Mexican oregano
- ¼ cup dried thyme
- 2 tablespoons freshly ground black pepper
- 2 tablespoons Morton kosher salt, plus more as needed
- 2 medium onions, roughly diced

Tamales

- ½ cup (100g) lard
- 4 cups (480g; loosely packed) masa harina, plus more as needed
- 1 tablespoon Morton kosher salt, plus more as needed
- 5 cups (1200g) beef stock, plus more as needed (preferably low-sodium)
- 20 to 30 dried corn husks
- Salsa Morita (page 248), for serving

Special Equipment

Stand mixer or electric hand mixer; tamalera (tamal steamer) or large pot with steamer basket/insert

How to Fill & Fold Tamales (Corn Husk)

Standard-issue beef tamales usually come filled with brisket or top round, which is great, but so is short rib, no? You can take the boy out of fine dining, but you can't take the fine dining out of the boy, m'right, Fermín? . . . Fermín?

1 **Make the filling:** Season the short ribs all over with the oregano, thyme, pepper, and salt. Fill the bottom of a tamalera or a pot with a steamer basket/insert with water. Arrange the onions in the steamer and place the seasoned short ribs on top of the onions. Set the steamer over medium-low heat, cover, and cook the short ribs until tender, 3 to 3½ hours, checking the water level periodically to be sure the steamer doesn't run dry and burn.

2 When the short ribs are cool enough to handle, remove the bones and shred the meat using your hands or 2 forks. Season to taste with salt and set aside.

3 **Make the masa:** In a stand mixer fitted with the paddle attachment, whip the lard on high speed (setting 10 on a KitchenAid) until light and fluffy. With the mixer on low speed (setting 2), add the masa harina and salt. Slowly add the beef stock. Mix until fully incorporated, scraping down the sides if necessary. (Alternatively, combine the ingredients in small batches using an electric hand mixer on low speed.) The masa should feel well hydrated (not gritty) with a creamy, airy texture that's easy to spread (think hummus or cake batter). If it's too dry, add more stock; if it's too wet, add more masa harina, whipping to incorporate. Taste and season with salt as needed. Set aside.

4 In a large bowl, combine the corn husks and enough hot water to cover. Soak the husks until soft, about 20 minutes. Gently wring out the husks and pat them dry with a kitchen towel.

5 **Assemble the tamales:** Working with one corn husk at a time, lay it on a work surface with the smooth side facing up and the wide end closest to you. Using a spoon, spatula, or bench scraper, spread a thin, even layer of masa (about ⅓ cup, depending on the size of the husk) from side to side, leaving the narrow end uncovered; you're looking to cover an area about 3 × 5 inches. Add ¼ cup of the shredded short ribs to the center of the masa. Fold the left side of the husk over the filling to cover it, then fold the right side so it overlaps the other side of the husk. Fold the pointy top down toward the bottom (wide) side of the husk, about halfway. Place on a plate or sheet pan, folded-side down. Repeat with the remaining husks, masa, and beef. Never done this before? Scan the QR code to see how.

6 **Steam the tamales:** Fill the bottom of a tamalera or a pot with steamer basket/insert with water. Place the tamales upright in the basket, with the open ends facing up. Cover and steam over medium-high heat for 55 minutes. Check for doneness by trying to pull the husk from a tamal; if it pulls away from the masa easily then they're ready!

7 Remove the pot from the heat and let the tamales rest, covered, for about 15 minutes. The tamales will firm up as they cool.

8 To serve, open the tamales and top with salsa morita.

Atoles

We know what some of you are thinking: What are two masa-based beverages doing in the tamales chapter? Surely this must be a rookie, mezcal-induced mistake! To this we say, "No manches, we are indeed coming correct." Tamales and atole are like french fries and soft serve—they just work. In fact, most reputable tamaleros, or tamal vendors, offer at least one, if not several, types of atoles to accompany their tamales, and you best believe the high pour makes it all taste that much better. Here, we've zeroed in on the classic flavors. Dunk or don't dunk your tamales in these atoles; chase or don't chase your tamales with these warm, comforting, spiced beverages—we'll still be out here getting our carb-on-carb swerve on because we just can't help ourselves.

Vanilla Atole

MAKES 7 CUPS

1½ cups masa harina

2½ tablespoons sugar, plus more as needed

2 cinnamon sticks (preferably Mexican canela)

1 tablespoon vanilla extract

Pinch of kosher salt

1 Fill a 5-quart saucepan with 7½ cups of water and bring to a boil over medium-high heat. Add the masa harina to the boiling water and reduce the heat to medium. Continuously whisk the mixture to prevent clumping until the masa harina is fully incorporated.

2 Add the sugar, cinnamon sticks, vanilla, and salt. With the heat still on medium, cook the mixture, whisking constantly to prevent it from burning, until it thickens enough to coat the back of a spoon (you're looking for a smooth, porridge-like consistency), 1 to 2 minutes. Taste, adding more sugar if desired and stirring to incorporate.

3 Remove the pot from the heat and allow the mixture to steep and cool for 10 minutes. Remove the cinnamon sticks.

4 Pour into mugs and serve warm. (While atole is best enjoyed immediately, it can be refrigerated in an airtight container for up to 24 hours. Add water as needed when reheating.)

Champurrado

MAKES 7 CUPS

1½ cups masa harina

1½ cups whole milk or oat milk (no sugar added)

2 (3-ounce) pieces stone-ground Mexican-style chocolate (such as Taza or Ibarra), or 6 ounces dark chocolate, chopped

5 tablespoons grated piloncillo or dark brown sugar

Pinch of kosher salt

2 cinnamon sticks (preferably Mexican canela)

1 Add the masa to a large saucepan and set over medium heat. Immediately add 6 cups of water in a slow, steady stream, whisking constantly to avoid lumps. When the masa is fully incorporated, bring it to a simmer and whisk in the milk, chocolate, piloncillo, and salt, stirring until the chocolate is melted, about 1 minute. Add the cinnamon sticks.

2 Remove the pot from the heat and allow the mixture to steep and cool for 10 minutes. Remove the cinnamon sticks.

3 Pour into mugs and serve warm. (While champurrado is best enjoyed immediately, it can be refrigerated in an airtight container for up to 24 hours. Add water as needed when reheating.)

Chocolate-Pecan Tamales

MAKES 20 TO 24 TAMALES

- 1 cup (2 sticks) unsalted butter, at room temperature
- ½ cup (155g) sweetened condensed milk, plus more for serving
- ½ cup (40g) unsweetened cocoa powder
- ⅓ cup (65g) sugar
- 1 tablespoon Morton kosher salt
- 2 teaspoons baking powder
- ½ teaspoon ground cinnamon
- 3 cups (360g; loosely packed) masa harina, plus more as needed
- 2 cups (500g) whole milk, plus more as needed
- 2 cups (500g) heavy cream
- 1 cup (120g) chopped 85% dark chocolate (such as La Rifa or Taza), in 1-inch rectangles
- ½ cup (60g) chopped pecans
- 20 banana leaves, tough middle ribs removed, cut into 9 × 12-inch rectangles
- Vanilla ice cream, for serving

Special Equipment

Stand mixer or electric hand mixer; tamalera (tamal steamer) or large pot with steamer basket/insert

How to Fill & Fold Tamales (Banana Leaf)

It isn't difficult to imagine this tamal being one of Moctezuma's favorite desserts back in the day. Adapted ever so slightly for the twenty-first century with a shot of condensed milk, a fistful of chopped pecans, and a scoop (or three) of vanilla ice cream, it gives flourless chocolate cake and brownie sundaes a run for their collective money. Unlike most modern-day Mexican sweets, this dessert skews slightly more savory, with a nutty, fudgy, dark-chocolatey finish that doesn't skimp on the decadence.

1. In a stand mixer fitted with the paddle attachment, combine the butter, condensed milk, cocoa powder, sugar, salt, baking powder, and cinnamon. Mix on medium speed (setting 5 or 6 on a KitchenAid) until all the ingredients are well incorporated and the mixture is fluffy. With the mixer still on medium, add the masa harina in 3 parts, allowing each part to fully incorporate before adding more. With the mixer on low speed (setting 2), slowly stream in the whole milk and cream until all the ingredients come together. (Alternatively, combine the ingredients in small batches using an electric hand mixer on low speed.) The masa should feel well hydrated (not gritty) with a smooth, almost pourable texture (think sour cream). If it's too dry, add more whole milk; if it's too wet, add more masa harina, whipping to incorporate. Fold in the chocolate and pecans. Set aside.

2. Heat a comal, griddle, or large skillet over medium-high heat and warm the banana leaves on both sides, 15 to 20 seconds per side, or until they turn a deep green color and become fragrant. Don't skip this step; it will make them pliable and prevent cracking or breaking.

3. Fill the middle of each banana leaf with about ½ cup of the prepared masa (depending on the size of the leaf). Fold the top and bottom sides of the leaf over the masa, then fold over the sides so that it looks like a rectangular present. Place seam-side down on a sheet pan or plate. Repeat with the remaining ingredients. Never done this before? Scan the QR code to see how.

4. Fill the bottom of a tamalera or a pot with steamer basket/insert with water. Place the tamales flat in the basket, staggering them on top of each other evenly in the pot. Cover and steam over medium-high heat for 45 minutes. Check for doneness by trying to pull the husk from a tamal; if it pulls away from the masa easily then they're ready!

5. Remove the pot from the heat and let the tamales rest, covered, for about 15 minutes. The tamales will firm up as they cool.

6. Open the tamales and serve drizzled with condensed milk and ice cream on the side.

Sweet Elote Tamales

MAKES 20 TO 24 TAMALES

- 1 cup (2 sticks) unsalted butter, at room temperature
- ¼ cup sugar
- ¼ cup honey
- ½ teaspoon Morton kosher salt
- 3 cups (360g; loosely packed) masa harina, plus more as needed
- 2 cups (500g) whole milk, plus more as needed
- 1 cup (250g) heavy cream
- 2 tablespoons vanilla extract
- 2 cups fresh sweet corn kernels (from about 2 ears)
- 20 to 24 dried corn husks

Special Equipment

Stand mixer or electric hand mixer; tamalera (tamal steamer) or large pot with steamer basket/insert

How to Fill & Fold Tamales (Corn Husk)

Fermín says: "These are like masa candy to me. They're not that deep, but they make for some delicious corn-on-corn action."

To his point, these tamales are quite simple. Nevertheless, it's worth noting that elote refers to both the savory street snack of corn on the cob (loaded with similar toppings as Esquites, page 33) as well as the corn kernels themselves, removed from the cob and featured in sweet dishes like this tamal or pan de elote, the Mexican equivalent of corn bread. To be sure, we're going for the latter here with sweet, yellow kernels of corn.

1 **Make the masa:** In a stand mixer fitted with the paddle attachment, combine the butter, sugar, honey, and salt, and mix on medium-high speed (setting 8 on a KitchenAid) until it is light and fluffy. With the mix er on medium speed (setting 5 or 6), add the masa harina in 3 parts, allowing each part to fully incorporate before adding more. With the mixer on low speed (setting 2), slowly stream in the milk, cream, and vanilla until fully combined. (Alternatively, combine the ingredients in small batches using an electric hand mixer on low speed.) The masa should feel well hydrated (not gritty) with a creamy, airy texture that's easy to spread (think hummus or cake batter). If it's too dry, add more whole milk; if it's too wet, add more masa harina, whipping to incorporate. Fold in the corn kernels. Set aside.

2 In a large bowl, combine the corn husks and enough hot water to cover. Soak the husks until soft, about 20 minutes. Gently wring out the husks and pat them dry with a kitchen towel.

3 **Assemble the tamales:** Working with one corn husk at a time, lay it on a work surface with the smooth side facing up and the wide end closest to you. Using a spoon, spatula, or bench scraper, spread a thin, even layer of the prepared masa (about ⅓ cup, depending on the size of the husk) from side to side, leaving the narrow end uncovered; you're looking to cover an area about 3 × 5 inches. Fold the left side of the husk over the filling to cover it, then fold the right side so it overlaps the other side of the husk. Fold the pointy top down toward the bottom (wide) side of the husk, about halfway. Place on a plate or sheet pan, folded-side down. Repeat with the remaining husks and masa. Never done this before? Scan the QR code to see how.

4 **Steam the tamales:** Fill the bottom of a tamalera or a pot with steamer basket/insert with water. Place the tamales upright in the basket, with the open ends facing up. Cover and steam over medium-high heat for 55 minutes. Check for doneness by trying to pull the husk from a tamal; if it pulls away from the masa easily then they're ready!

5 Remove the pot from the heat and let the tamales rest, covered, for about 15 minutes. The tamales will firm up as they cool.

6 To serve, open the tamales and enjoy warm.

Strawberry Tamales with Whipped Cream

MAKES 20 TO 24 TAMALES

Strawberry Tamales

- 1 cup hulled fresh strawberries
- 2 cups (500g) heavy cream, plus more if needed
- ½ cup (155g) sweetened condensed milk
- ½ cup (1 stick) unsalted butter, at room temperature
- ½ cup granulated sugar
- 1 tablespoon Morton kosher salt
- 3 cups (360g; loosely packed) masa harina, plus more as needed
- 20 to 30 banana leaves, tough middle ribs removed, cut into 9×12-inch rectangles

Toppings

- ¼ cup finely diced fresh strawberries
- ½ teaspoon granulated sugar
- Kosher salt
- Grated zest of 1 lemon
- 1 tablespoon fresh lemon juice
- 1 cup heavy cream
- ¼ cup confectioners' sugar

Special Equipment

Blender; stand mixer or electric hand mixer; tamalera (tamal steamer) or large pot with steamer basket/insert

How to Fill & Fold Tamales (Banana Leaf)

This is decidedly NOT the cloying, Barbie-pink strawberry tamal with tasteless rainbow nonpareils that Fermín grew up eating in Torreón, from which he still retains some mild culinary trauma. No, this is Chef Fermín giving Inner-Child Fermín a John Bradshaw–inspired, banana leaf–wrapped hug that says, "Everything es gonna be OK," after all. Onward.

1. **Make the masa:** In a blender, combine the hulled strawberries, cream, and condensed milk and blend until smooth. Set aside.
2. In a stand mixer fitted with the paddle attachment, combine the butter, granulated sugar, and salt. Beat on medium speed (setting 5 or 6 on a KitchenAid) until it is fluffy and well combined. With the mixer still on medium, add the masa harina in 3 parts, allowing each part to fully incorporate before adding more. With the mixer on low speed (setting 2), add the blended strawberry mixture and allow to fully incorporate. (Alternatively, combine the ingredients in small batches using an electric hand mixer on low speed.) The masa should feel well hydrated (not gritty) with a smooth, almost pourable texture (think sour cream). If it's too dry, add more heavy cream; if it's too wet, add more masa harina, whipping to incorporate. Set aside.
3. Heat a comal, griddle, or large skillet over medium-high heat and warm the banana leaves on both sides, 15 to 20 seconds per side, or until they turn a deep green color and become fragrant. Don't skip this step; it will make them pliable and prevent cracking or breaking.
4. **Assemble the tamales:** Fill the middle of each banana leaf with about ½ cup of the prepared masa (depending on the size of the leaf). Fold the top and bottom sides of the leaf over the masa, then fold over the sides so that it looks like a rectangular present. Place seam-side down on a sheet pan or plate. Repeat with the remaining ingredients. Never done this before? Scan the QR code to see how.
5. **Steam the tamales:** Fill the bottom of a tamalera or a pot with steamer basket/insert with water. Place the tamales flat in the basket, staggering them on top of each other evenly in the pot. Cover and steam over medium-high heat for 45 minutes. Check for doneness by trying to pull the husk from a tamal; if it pulls away from the masa easily then they're ready!
6. Remove the pot from the heat and let the tamales rest, covered, for about 15 minutes. The tamales will firm up as they cool.
7. **While tamales are cooking, make the toppings:** In a small bowl, stir together the diced strawberries, granulated sugar, a pinch of salt, and the lemon zest and juice, then set aside.
8. In a stand mixer fitted with the whisk, combine the cream and confectioners' sugar and whip on low speed (setting 2 on a KitchenAid) and gradually increase up to high speed (setting 10) until soft peaks form, 6 to 7 minutes.
9. To serve, open the tamales while warm and top with the whipped cream and macerated strawberries.

Nestlé
La Lechera
La Original
desde 1910
Sweetened
Condensed Milk
Leche Condensada
Azucarada
NET WT/PESO NETO 14 OZ (397 g)

Roasted Sweet Potato Tamales with Spiced Pepitas

MAKES 14 TAMALES

Spiced Pepitas

- 1 cup raw pumpkin seeds
- 2 tablespoons olive oil
- 2 tablespoons dark brown sugar
- ½ teaspoon Morton kosher salt
- ¼ teaspoon cayenne pepper
- Pinch of ground cinnamon

Tamales

- 3 medium sweet potatoes, scrubbed clean, or 3 cups canned pumpkin
- ½ cup (1 stick) unsalted butter, cut into 8 tablespoons
- ⅓ cup (75g) refined coconut oil
- 3 cups (360g; loosely packed) masa harina, plus more as needed
- 1 teaspoon baking powder
- ½ teaspoon Morton kosher salt
- ¼ teaspoon baking soda
- 2 cups (500g) whole milk, plus more as needed
- 2 cups (500g) heavy cream
- ¼ cup agave syrup
- 14 banana leaves, tough middle ribs removed, cut into 9 × 12-inch rectangles
- Sweetened condensed milk, for serving

Special Equipment

Stand mixer or electric hand mixer; tamalera (tamal steamer) or large pot with steamer basket/insert

The shrill whistle of the camote vendor signals something sweet is on its way: roasted sweet potato drizzled with sweetened condensed milk. An iconic street food in their own right, camotes, or roasted sweet potatoes, are the base of this stunning dessert tamal recipe courtesy of chef Sarah Thompson of Casa Playa restaurant in Las Vegas. This version has been adapted slightly with the home cook in mind, so you'll have to taste the original for yourself in Sin City next time you're feeling lucky. Don't skip the spiced pepitas; they add crucial sweetness and crunch.

1. **Make the spiced pepitas:** Preheat the oven to 400°F. Line a sheet pan with parchment paper.

2. In a medium bowl, combine the pumpkin seeds, olive oil, brown sugar, salt, cayenne, and cinnamon, and stir until combined.

3. Spread the spiced pepitas on the lined pan. Roast until the pepitas are fully toasted and the sugar is melted and caramelized, 10 to 15 minutes, stirring at the halfway mark. Don't turn that oven off! Remove the pan and let the pepitas cool before setting aside or storing in an airtight container.

4. **Make the masa:** If using canned pumpkin, move on to the next step (and you can turn the oven off). If using sweet potatoes, with the oven still at 400°F, line the sheet pan with a fresh piece of parchment. Poke holes through the skin of the sweet potatoes all over using a fork or sharp knife. Place the sweet potatoes on the sheet pan and bake until the skin is dried and crunchy and the insides are very tender (no resistance when poked with a sharp knife or fork into the middle), 50 minutes to 1 hour. Allow the sweet potatoes to cool, then peel and mash into a smooth puree using a potato masher or fork.

5. In a skillet (preferably a stainless-steel or light-colored skillet so you can see the butter change color more easily) over medium heat, melt the butter. Swirl the pan occasionally so the butter melts evenly. Watch closely as it begins to bubble and foam; it will change color from yellow to golden, and then, when the foam subsides, to a toasty brown. When the butter smells nutty and delicious, and reaches a light brown color, immediately take the pan off the heat and transfer the butter to a heatproof bowl and let sit until cool to the touch. (If you want to do this step ahead, the browned butter will keep in a glass jar at room temperature for 5 days or in the fridge for up to 2 weeks.)

RECIPE CONTINUES →

How to Fill & Fold Tamales (Banana Leaf)

6. In a stand mixer fitted with the paddle attachment, whip the coconut oil on medium-high speed (setting 8 on a KitchenAid) until it is light and fluffy. Slowly add the browned butter in 3 batches, making sure it is fully combined and the same consistency as the coconut oil before adding the next batch. Continue to whip until light and airy. With the mixer on medium-low speed (setting 4), add the masa harina in 3 parts, allowing each part to fully incorporate before adding more, followed by the baking powder, salt, and baking soda, scraping down the sides, if necessary. Slowly stream in the whole milk, followed by the cream and the agave, and mix until fully incorporated. Lastly, with the mixer on high speed (setting 10), add the mashed sweet potato or pumpkin and mix until fully incorporated. (Alternatively, combine the ingredients in small batches using an electric hand mixer on low speed.) The masa should feel well hydrated (not gritty) with a smooth, almost pourable texture (think sour cream). If it's too dry, add more whole milk; if it's too wet, add more masa harina, whipping to incorporate.

7. **Assemble the tamales:** Heat a comal, griddle, or large skillet over medium-high heat and warm the banana leaves on both sides, 15 to 20 seconds per side, or until they turn a deep green color and become fragrant. Don't skip this step; it will make them pliable and prevent cracking or breaking.

8. Fill the middle of each banana leaf with about ½ cup of the prepared masa (depending on the size of the leaf). Fold the top and bottom sides of the leaf over the masa, then fold over the sides so that it looks like a rectangular present. Place seam-side down on a sheet pan or plate. Repeat with the remaining ingredients. Never done this before? Scan the QR code to see how.

9. **Steam the tamales:** Fill the bottom of a tamalera or a pot with steamer basket/insert with water. Place the tamales flat in the basket, staggering them on top of each other evenly in the pot. Cover and steam over medium-high heat for 1 hour. Check for doneness by trying to pull the husk from a tamal; if it pulls away from the masa easily then they're ready!

10. Remove the pot from the heat and let the tamales rest, covered, for about 15 minutes. The tamales will firm up as they cool.

11. Open the tamales while warm or at room temperature and serve with a drizzle of the condensed milk and a sprinkle of the spiced pepitas on top.

TODO LO
DEMÁS

Everything else

All of us, even the most obsessively organized individuals reading this, have a drawer in our homes, offices, or cars where we stuff all the stuff that doesn't thematically go with the other stuffs. This chapter is that drawer, for todo lo demás, or everything else.

In this particular drawer, we have dishes that correspond to the letter *T* like tlayudas (pages 190 to 193) and tlacoyos (pages 207 to 211), but they don't quite add up to being enough for their own dedicated chapter. We have other dishes that do not start with the letter *T* but have been canonized by street vendors across Mexico and are therefore vitamina T in spirit, if not in name. And finally, at least one other dish is included in this chapter that neither starts with *T* nor is even considered a street food per se, but seemed like a worthwhile addition by our editorial brain trust.

We invite you to this motley crew of Mexican classics that are in a league of their own, just like Geena Davis.

Tlayuditas

MAKES 4 TLAYUDITAS

¾ cup (90g; packed) masa harina, plus more as needed

Scant ¾ cup (170g) warm (but not hot) water, plus more as needed

Special Equipment

Tortilla press and plastic liners

How to Make Tlayuditas

Tlayudas are large-format tortillas, often upwards of 13 inches in diameter and hailing from the state of Oaxaca. But they're not just any old large-format tortillas, and they certainly are nothing like tortillas for burritos: They actually refer to a specific level of doneness of the tortilla itself. Somewhere texturally between a tortilla blanda, or corn tortilla (see page 97), and a comal-cooked tostada (see page 29) lives the tlayuda. Despite having the chew of a somewhat stale tortilla, it is the Goldilocks of tortillas when it comes to the functions of filling it, folding it, and roasting it ever so slightly over charcoal until it becomes the crispy, eponymous street food dish that it (also) is. Since tlayuda presses are hard to come by, you can use a tortilla press to achieve the desired tlayuda texture in a diminutive form.

1. Add the masa harina to a medium bowl. Working by hand, mix in the warm water, kneading the dough until the water is fully incorporated and there are no dry spots. Don't worry about overworking the dough—corn has no gluten, so knead to your heart's content. The masa should be moist to the touch but not tacky (leaving bits of wet masa on your hand and fingers). If it's too wet, add a bit more masa harina; if too dry, add a bit more water.
2. Divide the masa into 4 balls about the size of a golf ball and set aside.
3. Preheat a large comal, griddle, or large skillet over medium-high heat.
4. Using a tortilla press lined with plastic on both sides, press a ball of masa to flatten, then open the press and turn the masa 180 degrees. Close and press again to form a flat, large, round shape slightly thicker than a tortilla, about ⅛ inch thick and 6 inches in diameter.
5. Reduce the heat under the comal to medium. Carefully remove the plastic liner, then gently lay the tlayuda down on the comal in a sweeping, backhanded motion. Cook one side of the tlayuda for about 60 seconds. We're cooking it longer than a tortilla, since it's both thicker and we're aiming for a dryer texture (somewhere in between a tortilla and a tostada).
6. When the edges of the tlayuda start to curl up, flip the tlayuda, then cook for another 60 seconds. Flipping back and forth, continue to cook for 15 to 20 seconds on each side until the tlayuda is able to fold with a little bit of resistance but not so much resistance that once folded it cracks. The whole process takes 7 to 8 minutes. Transfer the tlayuda to a plate.
7. Repeat with the remaining masa balls, reusing the same plastic liners, and if not eating immediately, store in an airtight container for up to 3 days. Scan the QR code to see how it's done.

Beef Tasajo Tlayuditas

MAKES 4 TLAYUDITAS

- 8 ounces top round steak, cut into 8 thin slices (about ⅛ inch)
- Kosher salt
- 3 tablespoons lard, melted
- 4 Tlayuditas (page 190)
- ¼ cup Asiento (page 255)
- ¼ cup Smoky Refried Beans (page 238, made with black beans), warmed
- 2 cups (loosely packed) hand-pulled strands quesillo (a.k.a. queso Oaxaca), or 1½ cups shredded low-moisture mozzarella
- Shredded iceberg lettuce, for garnish

For Serving

- Lime wedges
- Salsa de Chile de Árbol (page 250)
- Salsa de Molcajete (page 251)

Special Equipment

- Charcoal or gas grill or grill pan

Now that you know what a tlayuda is, let's talk about tasajo. Tasajo appears in several Latin cultures, as the word simply translates to "a piece of meat," and as a result it assumes various forms. For example, little Jorge grew up in Miami, where tasajo most often refers to the Cuban dish of dried, cured, shredded beef served with a healthy side of congri (black beans and rice). In Mexico, where little Fermín grew up, tasajo most often refers to salted and air-dried beef, though technically it can be any kind of meat. There, it is cooked to an almost jerky-like consistency, making it a perfect option for the American baby boomers of the world (hello, in-laws!) who live on the extra-well-done side of life.

1. Arrange the steak on a sheet pan and generously season the meat with salt on both sides (don't be afraid!), then brush both sides with the lard. For best results, let the beef rest, uncovered, in the fridge for 2 to 4 hours before grilling.
2. Prepare a gas or charcoal grill (preferably charcoal) to high heat. Grill the meat about 2 minutes per side, until fully cooked with a crispy char on the exterior. (Alternatively, cook the meat in a grill pan or skillet on the stovetop.)
3. Warm the tlayuditas on the grill, then place them on plates. Spread 1 tablespoon of the asiento on each tlayudita, then follow with the beans and quesillo, and garnish with the shredded lettuce. Finally, top each with 2 pieces of the beef. Serve with the lime wedges and the salsas on the side.

Steak Enchilada Tlayuditas

MAKES 4 TLAYUDITAS

- 6 guajillo chiles, stemmed, seeded, and veins removed
- 2 chiles de árbol, stemmed
- ½ large onion, roughly chopped
- 5 garlic cloves, peeled
- ½ cup distilled white vinegar
- 2 tablespoons Morton kosher salt, plus more as needed
- 8 ounces top round steak, cut into 8 thin slices (⅛ inch thick)
- Neutral oil
- 4 Tlayuditas (page 190)
- ¼ cup Asiento (page 255)
- ¼ cup Smoky Refried Beans (page 238, made with black beans), warmed
- 2 cups (loosely packed) hand-pulled strands quesillo (a.k.a. queso Oaxaca), or 1½ cups shredded low-moisture mozzarella
- Shredded iceberg lettuce (optional), for garnish
- Lime wedges, for squeezing
- Salsa Taquera (page 246), for garnish

Special Equipment

Blender; charcoal or gas grill or grill pan

This recipe is inspired by cecina enchilada, our go-to tlayuda order whenever we're in Oaxaca. Cecina, which translates to salted, dried meat, can mean different things depending on which part of Mexico you're in. For this particular dish, we will be leading with thinly cut beef that is coated in chile adobo (that's the "enchilada"). Like tasajo, the meat is thinly cut, preferably cooked over charcoal, and served well done.

1. In a medium bowl, combine the guajillo and árbol chiles and enough warm water to cover. Soak the chiles for 10 to 15 minutes to soften.
2. Drain the chiles, reserving ¼ cup of the soaking liquid, then transfer the chiles to a blender. Add the soaking liquid and puree. Add the onion, garlic, vinegar, and salt, and puree the marinade until smooth.
3. On a sheet pan, arrange the slices of beef and season both sides with salt, then brush both sides with the marinade. (You'll end up using about half of the marinade. Extra marinade keeps in the fridge for 7 to 10 days or in the freezer for up to 3 weeks, and is delicious on any grilled meat.) For best results, let the meat air-dry in the fridge for 2 to 4 hours before grilling.
4. Prepare a gas or charcoal grill (preferably charcoal) to high heat. Lightly oil the grates and grill the meat for about 2 minutes per side, until fully cooked with a crispy char and caramelized deep-red color on the exterior. (Alternatively, cook the meat in a grill pan or skillet on the stovetop.)
5. Warm the tlayuditas on the grill, then place them on plates. Spread 1 tablespoon of the asiento on each tlayudita, then follow with refried beans, quesillo, and shredded lettuce (if using). Finally, top each with 2 pieces of the beef. Serve with lime wedges and the salsa on the side.

Bean and Cheese Sopes

MAKES 4 SOPES

1½ cups (180g; packed) masa harina, plus more as needed

Scant 1½ cups (340g) warm (but not hot) water, plus more as needed

1 cup Smoky Refried Beans (page 238, made with black beans), warmed

½ cup Salsa de Chicharrón (page 248)

½ cup crumbled queso fresco

Mexican crema, for garnish

Special Equipment

Tortilla press and plastic liners

How to Make Sopes

Here is where things start to get especially confusing from a taxonomic standpoint, and thereby inherently, charmingly Mexican. Only in Mexico do you find culinary staples that go by myriad names, depending on what part of the country you find yourself in.

Observe:
"Yey, sopes!"
"Those aren't sopes, they're pescadillas!"
"No manches, they're memelas!"
"Y'all are insane. These are garnachas, and everyone here knows it."

Okay, this doesn't *just* happen in Mexico, but it seems to happen a lot more there—certainly more passionately so—than in most other places around the world (see: Carrot and Potato Tacos Dorados, page 132). To be sure, sopes, like the ones we have highlighted in this recipe, are thick masa pancakes with a raised outer ridge meant for retaining toppings. Anything goes when it comes to such toppings, but we find some combination of beans, salsa, and cheese to always be a winning choice.

1. Add the masa harina to a medium bowl. Working by hand, mix in the warm water, kneading the dough until the water is fully incorporated and there are no dry spots. Don't worry about overworking the dough—corn has no gluten, so knead to your heart's content. The masa should be moist to the touch but not tacky (leaving bits of wet masa on your hand and fingers). If it's too wet, add a bit more masa harina; if too dry, add a bit more water.
2. Preheat a comal, griddle, or large skillet over medium heat.
3. Divide the masa into 4 equal portions, rolling each into a ball. Using your hands or a tortilla press lined with plastic on both sides, flatten the masa balls into disks about ¼ inch thick.
4. Place the disks on the comal without overlapping (depending on the size of your comal, you may want to work in batches) and cook on each side, flipping when they easily slide across the pan when you touch the top and a crust has formed on the bottom, about 3 minutes per side.
5. Remove from the heat and let cool briefly. When slightly—but not entirely—cooled, pinch the edges and create a "barrier" or ridge around the circumference to form a sope that allows all the fillings to remain on the inside. (Careful not to burn your fingers!) If the masa inside still feels pretty raw after pinching, return the sope to the comal over medium heat, ridge-side down, to cook for about 1 minute longer. Never done this before? Scan the QR code to see how.
6. To assemble the sopes, top each of them with equal amounts of the refried black beans, salsa, and queso fresco. Garnish with a drizzle of crema.

Squash Blossom Quesadillas with Oaxacan Cheese

MAKES 4 QUESADILLAS

- 16 fresh squash blossoms
- Neutral oil
- 4 corn tortillas, homemade (page 97) or store-bought
- 3 cups (loosely packed) hand-pulled strands quesillo (a.k.a. queso Oaxaca), or 2¼ cups shredded low-moisture mozzarella
- 8 fresh epazote leaves
- Salsa Verde Cruda (page 249), for serving

If you were to order a quesadilla in Oaxaca, such as this classic rendition with squash blossoms and epazote, you'd bet that it would come with cheese—quesillo, to be exact. If you were to order a quesadilla in Mexico City, however, cheese would not necessarily be a given; you'd have to specify your order and your cheese (quesillo or queso fresco) accordingly. Suffice it to say, there are subtle regional differences between even the humblest of dishes, including this quesadilla right here. Whereas Mexico City–style squash blossom quesadillas would feature the flowers in a sautéed or guisado form, flowers in the Oaxacan style are gently steamed inside the quesadilla itself. In our humblest of opinions, squash blossoms don't really taste like much either way. They do, however, add a delicate leafy texture for a mild contrast in bite, and they are objectively gorgeous to behold in this context, especially with a peppery pop of vibrant green epazote in the mix. If you can't find fresh epazote, basil (while different in flavor) pairs nicely with the squash blossoms.

1. To clean the squash blossoms, use tweezers or small kitchen scissors to remove the stamen (the bright orange bulb found inside the flower). Peel the blossoms into individual petals, discarding the stems.
2. Preheat a lightly oiled comal, griddle, or large skillet over medium-low heat. Place the tortillas on the comal without overlapping to warm (depending on the size of your comal, you may want to work in batches). Flip them so the warmed side is facing up, and evenly top each one with one-fourth of the cheese.
3. When the cheese begins to melt, evenly top each tortilla with a few squash blossom petals (each tortilla should get the equivalent of 4 full blossoms, which may look like a lot, but they will shrink significantly in the cooking process).
4. When the blossoms have begun to shrink, top each tortilla with 2 epazote leaves and fold the tortillas over to create a half-moon shape. Cook for another minute to fully melt the cheese and create a bit of a crispy crust on the outside of the tortilla.
5. Remove from the heat and serve with the salsa.

Huitlacoche Quesadillas

MAKES 4 QUESADILLAS

- Neutral oil
- ¾ cup corn kernels (from 1 ear)
- ½ cup diced onion (about ½ medium)
- 10 ounces fresh huitlacoche (about 3½ loosely packed cups)
- Kosher salt
- 4 corn tortillas, homemade (page 97) or store-bought
- 3 cups (loosely packed) hand-pulled strands quesillo (a.k.a. queso Oaxaca), or 2¼ cups shredded low-moisture mozzarella
- Salsa Roja (page 244), for serving

Huitlacoche is to quesadillas as white truffles are to pasta—a delicacy rich in earthy, indulgent umami—but at what is typically a fraction of the cost. Sometimes known as cuitlacoche or corn smut, huitlacoche is a fungus that grows on maize and causes the kernels to turn gray and swell in size. While it can and will occur naturally in the right (or wrong, depending on what your farming goals are) growing conditions, most commercially available huitlacoche comes from inoculated crops that have been cultivated in controlled agricultural settings. Fresh huitlacoche is quite perishable, which can sometimes make sourcing it a challenge. If your local Mexican grocer doesn't carry it, some reputable online companies like Huitla do offer a high-quality product, but note that pricing can get expensive with the expedited shipping it requires. Though not ideal, canned huitlacoche can also be doctored and used in a pinch.

1. Set a medium sauté pan over medium heat and add enough oil to lightly coat the bottom. Add the corn and onion and cook until translucent, about 5 minutes. Add the huitlacoche and cook, stirring constantly, until the huitlacoche starts to darken in color and shrink. Season to taste with salt and set aside.
2. Preheat a lightly oiled comal, griddle, or large skillet over medium-low heat. Place the tortillas on the comal without overlapping to warm (depending on the size of your comal, you may want to work in batches). Flip them so the warmed sides are facing up, and top each with one-quarter of the cheese.
3. When the cheese begins to melt, top each tortilla with the huitlacoche mixture. Fold the tortillas over to create a half-moon shape and cook for another minute to fully melt the cheese and create a bit of a crispy crust on the outside.
4. Remove from the heat and serve with the salsa on the side or open the quesadillas back up and spoon some salsa inside.

Elote and Crab Huaraches

MAKES 4 HUARACHES

- 1½ cups (180g; packed) masa harina, plus more as needed
- Scant 1½ cups (340g) warm (but not hot) water, plus more as needed
- Neutral oil
- 1 cup finely diced onion (about 1 medium)
- 1 cup finely diced fresh Hatch or poblano chiles (about 2 chiles)
- 1 cup corn kernels (from about 1½ ears)
- 2 garlic cloves, thinly sliced
- 1 teaspoon minced jalapeño chile
- ½ cup heavy cream
- ½ package (4 ounces) cream cheese
- 1 (12-ounce or 1-pound) can crabmeat (depending on availability)
- Minced cilantro stems, for garnish
- Lemon wedges, for serving

Special Equipment

- Tortilla press and plastic liners

How to Make Huaraches

If we're being honest about the genesis of this dish, Fermín was crab fishing during an all-expenses-paid trip in Alaska with a bunch of chef friends, and I, Jorge, came down with a mild case of envy. At the time, my coping mechanism was to vulnerably request a crab huarache recipe for this chapter. The result has since gone on to become one of my favorite dishes in this cookbook because (1) it's a banger of a dish, and (2) acts of service are one of my love languages. The huarache gets its name from the woven leather sandals commonly worn throughout Mexico and is loosely reminiscent of one's sole. Toppings abound, but this particular treatment is nothing traditional. There's more Massachusetts than Michoacán happening in each bite—but in a *Marta's* Vineyard sort of way, if you know what we mean. If you've never used cilantro stems to garnish before, you're in for a delightfully crunchy treat.

1. Add the masa harina to a medium bowl. Working by hand, mix in the warm water, kneading the dough until the water is fully incorporated and there are no dry spots. Don't worry about overworking the dough—corn has no gluten, so knead to your heart's content. It should be moist to the touch but not tacky (leaving bits of wet masa on your hand and fingers). If it's too wet, add a bit more masa harina; if too dry, add a bit more water. Cover with a damp paper towel until ready to use.
2. In a medium skillet over medium-low heat, warm 1½ tablespoons of oil. Add the onion, chiles, corn, garlic, and jalapeño. Cook, stirring occasionally, until the vegetables begin to soften, about 2 minutes.
3. Increase the heat to medium and add the cream and cream cheese. Cook, stirring occasionally, until the cream cheese melts and the cream slightly thickens, about 5 minutes. Turn off the heat and gently fold in the crabmeat with a spatula.
4. Divide the masa into 4 equal balls and shape them into 6-inch-long logs. Using a tortilla press lined with plastic on both sides, lightly press a log of masa to form an oval about ½ inch thick. Repeat with the remaining logs of masa, reusing the same plastic liners. Never done this before? Scan the QR code to see how.
5. On a lightly oiled comal, griddle, or large skillet over medium heat, cook the huaraches without overlapping (depending on the size of your comal, you may want to work in batches) until the masa is firm and cooked through, about 1½ minutes per side. Transfer to a plate.
6. Spoon a generous amount of the crab mixture onto each huarache and garnish with the cilantro. Serve with lemon wedges on the side.

Requesón Tetelas

MAKES 6 TETELAS

- 2 cups (240g; packed) masa harina, plus more as needed
- Scant 2 cups (455g) warm (but not hot) water, plus more as needed
- ¾ to 1¼ cups Requesón (recipe follows) or store-bought ricotta
- 6 fresh epazote leaves (optional)
- Neutral oil, for frying (optional)

Special Equipment

Tortilla press and plastic liners

How to Make Tetelas

Tetelas may not be a ubiquitous street food in Mexico [*yet*], but they are made of masa and happen to start with the letter *T*, so here they are. Tetelas are essentially tortillas that have been stuffed with filling and folded into a neat little triangular empanada, somewhat reminiscent of a crepe. Their name comes from the combination of Nahuatl words tetl ("hill") and tla ("many"), as in "place of many hills," and their shape indeed bears some resemblance to a one-dimensional hill or mountain. This recipe calls for homemade requesón, which is the Mexican equivalent of ricotta. If you'd prefer opting for store-bought ricotta, though, we won't judge; just be sure to drain it a bit before filling your tetelas.

1 Add the masa harina to a large bowl. Working by hand, mix in the warm water, kneading the dough until the water is fully incorporated and there are no dry spots. Don't worry about overworking the dough—corn has no gluten, so knead to your heart's content. It should be moist to the touch but not tacky (leaving bits of wet masa on your hand and fingers). If it's too wet, add a bit more masa harina; if too dry, add a bit more water.

2 Divide the masa into 6 equal portions, rolling each into a ball. Using a tortilla press lined with plastic on both sides, press a ball of masa to form a tortilla about ¼ inch thick and 7 inches in diameter.

3 With the tortilla still on the press, remove the top liner and place 2 to 3 tablespoons of the requesón in the center of the tortilla. Top the requesón with an epazote leaf (if using).

4 Using the bottom plastic liner, fold the tortilla from the upper left diagonally toward the center, then from the upper right toward the center, and finally from the bottom up toward the center to create a sealed triangle. Set aside. Never done this before? Scan the QR code to see how it's done. Repeat with the remaining dough, requesón, and epazote (if using), reusing the same plastic liners.

5 Heat a comal, griddle, or large skillet over medium heat. Working in batches if needed, cook the tetelas seam-side up for 2 to 3 minutes, or until lightly golden. Flip and cook on the other side for 2 to 3 more minutes, or until the masa is cooked through. (Alternatively, for a crispier texture, fry them in 1 teaspoon of oil in a large skillet.) Serve while warm.

RECIPE CONTINUES →

Requesón

MAKES 1¼ POUNDS

- 1 gallon full-fat creamline (cream-top) milk
- ½ cup distilled white vinegar or lemon juice
- 1 tablespoon Morton kosher salt, plus more as needed

Special Equipment

- Candy/deep-fry thermometer (optional)

Requesón is a fresh cheese similar to ricotta but firmer. It is delicious spread atop any plain tostada, whether baked, fried, or from the comal (see pages 27 to 29) with a hit of Salsa Macha (page 252) or on a buñuelo (page 231) with a drizzle of honey.

1. In a large soup pot over medium heat, warm the milk, stirring occasionally to prevent it from scorching. Do not allow it to boil or scald. Clip a candy/deep-fry thermometer to the side of the pot and warm the milk until the temperature reaches 185°F. (This can take up to 1 hour 15 minutes.) Remove the pot from the heat.
2. Slowly stir in the vinegar. The milk will begin to curdle immediately. Let the mixture sit for 10 minutes to allow the curds to separate from the whey.
3. Line a colander with cheesecloth and set it in the sink. Gently pour the milk mixture into the colander. The whey will drain through, leaving the curds in the colander. Sprinkle the salt over the curds and stir gently to combine. Taste and season with more salt as needed.
4. Draw the edges of the cheesecloth together and tie them together to form a bag. Thread the handle of a wooden spoon through the knot and hang the bag over the sink or a bowl to drain for about 2 hours, or until it reaches a consistency that resembles cream cheese. Transfer the requesón to an airtight container and store in the fridge until ready to use, up to 5 days.

Hoja Santa Tetelas with Refried Black Beans and Cheese

MAKES 6 TETELAS

2 cups (240g; packed) masa harina, plus more as needed

Scant 2 cups (455g) warm (but not hot) water, plus more as needed

6 fresh hoja santa leaves

¾ cup Smoky Refried Beans (page 238, made with black beans)

6 cups (loosely packed) hand-pulled strands quesillo (a.k.a. queso Oaxaca), or 4½ cups shredded low-moisture mozzarella

Neutral oil

Salsa Morita (page 248), for serving

Special Equipment

Tortilla press and plastic liners

How to Make Tetelas

It's hard to talk about tetelas without talking about Itanoní, a Michelin-mentioned masa institution in Oaxaca whose Nahuatl name translates to "flower of corn." Sure, tetelas were around well before this chef's haunt of a restaurant opened in 2001, but Itanoní arguably played the biggest role in popularizing these triangular stuffed masa pockets on restaurant menus throughout Mexico and beyond. This particular version pays homage to its tetela espirituosa, or spiritual tetela, and it doesn't deviate at all from the original, save for local ingredient sourcing.

There is no recommended substitution here for fresh hoja santa, also known as root beer plant, and we'd like to say sorry about that. We recipe-tested dried hoja santa leaves, which are readily available online, but they just don't have that same bright anise-like flavor that makes this original dish so . . . divine. Thus, feel free to skip this one entirely if you're unable to track down fresh hoja santa or simply go without it, because there's absolutely nothing wrong with beans and cheese in a tetela.

1. Add the masa harina to a large bowl. Working by hand, mix in the warm water, kneading the dough until the water is fully incorporated and there are no dry spots. Don't worry about overworking the dough—corn has no gluten, so knead to your heart's content. It should be moist to the touch but not tacky (leaving bits of wet masa on your hand and fingers). If it's too wet, add a bit more masa harina; if too dry, add a bit more water.

2. Divide the dough into 6 equal portions, rolling each into a ball. Using a tortilla press lined with plastic on both sides, place an hoja santa leaf on the bottom of the tortilla press with the smooth side facing down. Place a masa ball on top, then press to form a tortilla about ¼ inch thick.

3. With the tortilla still on the press, remove the top liner and place 2 tablespoons of the refried black beans in the center of the tortilla, leaving at least 1 inch around the circumference. Top the beans with one-sixth of the quesillo, spreading it as flat as possible.

4. Using the bottom plastic liner, fold the tortilla from the upper left diagonally toward the center, then from the upper right toward the center, and finally from the bottom up toward the center to create a sealed triangle. Transfer to a plate. Never done this before? Scan the QR code to see how. Repeat with the remaining masa balls, hoja santa leaves, beans, and quesillo, reusing the same plastic liners.

5. Heat a lightly oiled comal, griddle, or large skillet over medium-low heat. Working in batches if needed, cook the tetelas seam-side up for 2 to 3 minutes, until you start to smell the hoja santa. Flip and cook on the other side for 2 more minutes, or until the masa is cooked through. Serve warm with the salsa.

Black Bean Tlacoyos with Queso Fresco and Crema

MAKES 4 TLACOYOS

- 1½ cups (180g; packed) masa harina, plus more as needed
- Scant 1½ cups (340g) warm (but not hot) water, plus more as needed
- 1 cup Smoky Refried Beans (page 238, made with black beans)

Garnishes

- Salsa Verde Cruda (page 249)
- Crumbled queso fresco
- Mexican crema
- Minced cilantro
- Diced white onion

Special Equipment

- Tortilla press and plastic liners

How to Make Tlacoyos

Don't let the limited selection of tlacoyo recipes in this cookbook fool you: We adore these football-shaped, bean-filled masa turnovers like Luís loved Mariah and Jennifer loved Ben. We especially fall for them when they're slightly crispy on the outside and molten on the inside—just like we were after eating nothing but tacos for seventy-two hours in Mexico City during our first *Vitamina T* cookbook photo shoot—but we'll really take them however we can get them. While the pros can and will shape tlacoyos entirely by hand, we call for a hybrid (tortilla) press-and-fold method for ours.

1. Add the masa harina to a medium bowl. Working by hand, mix in the warm water, kneading the dough until the water is fully incorporated and there are no dry spots. Don't worry about overworking the dough—corn has no gluten, so knead to your heart's content. It should be moist to the touch but not tacky (leaving bits of wet masa on your hand and fingers). If it's too wet, add a bit more masa harina; if too dry, add a bit more water.
2. Divide the masa into 4 equal portions, rolling each into a ball. Using a tortilla press lined with plastic on both sides, press a ball of masa to form a tortilla with a 7-inch diameter.
3. With the tortilla still on the press, remove the top liner and spread about ¼ cup of the refried black beans in a log shape in the center of the tortilla, leaving plenty of room around the circumference.
4. Using the bottom plastic liner, fold the left side onto the middle of the tortilla, then the right, like an envelope. Next, use the liner to nudge the top right side diagonally downward to meet the upper middle, and repeat with the left side. Do the same on the bottom right and left, nudging them diagonally upward to create an oval, or football-shaped, masa pocket to fully encase the filling. Use the top liner to gently smooth out any folds and creases that might occur from the folding. Transfer to a plate. Never done this before? Scan the QR code to see how. Repeat with the remaining masa balls and beans, reusing the same plastic liners.
5. Heat a dry comal, griddle, or large skillet over medium heat. Add the tlacoyos seam-side up and cook until the masa is fully cooked and achieves a bit of a char on both sides, 4 to 6 minutes per side.
6. To serve, generously spread the salsa over each tlacoyo. Garnish with the queso fresco, crema, cilantro, and onion.

Vitamina T(ip)

This is an excellent recipe to parcook, freeze, and reheat for breakfast, lunch, or dinner.

Fava Bean Tlacoyos with Nopalitos

MAKES 4 TLACOYOS

- ⅔ cup dried peeled fava beans
- Neutral oil
- 1 cup finely diced fresh nopal (cactus paddle) with spines carefully removed (from 1 paddle; see Tip)
- ½ cup minced onion (about ¼ large)
- ½ cup finely diced ripe tomato (about 1 Roma)
- 1 serrano chile, stemmed, seeded, and finely diced
- Kosher salt
- 3 tablespoons grated Cotija cheese
- 2 teaspoons nutritional yeast
- 1 garlic clove, minced
- 1½ cups (180g; packed) masa harina, plus more as needed
- Scant 1½ cups (340g) warm (but not hot) water, plus more as needed
- Crumbled queso fresco, for garnish

Special Equipment

Tortilla press and plastic liners

How to Make Tlacoyos

Few dishes feel quite as connected to the CDMX street food experience as fava-filled tlacoyos and nopal, or cactus paddle, salsa. While tlacoyos (stuffed masa turnovers) have been a prized itacate, or to-go food, since Mesoamerican times, the fava beans, introduced to the New World by the Spanish, are a relatively contemporary twist on the theme.

1. In a 2-quart saucepan, combine the fava beans with about 4 cups of water. Bring to a boil over high heat, then reduce to a simmer and cook over medium heat until the beans are tender, about 45 minutes, adding more water as needed to keep the beans covered while cooking.
2. Meanwhile, in a large sauté pan over medium warm, heat 1½ tablespoons of oil. Add the nopal, onion, tomato, and chile, and sauté until the nopal is tender and the juices it releases have evaporated, 6 to 8 minutes. Season to taste with salt and set the salsa aside.
3. Drain the cooked beans and place them in a large bowl. Add the cheese, nutritional yeast, and garlic. Using a potato masher or the back of a fork, lightly mash the beans and mix the ingredients until well combined. The mixture may appear crumbly. Taste and season with salt as needed then set aside.
4. Add the masa harina to a medium bowl. Working by hand, mix in the water, kneading the dough until the water is fully incorporated and there are no dry spots. It should be moist to the touch but not tacky (leaving bits of wet masa on your hand and fingers). If it's too wet, add a bit more masa harina; if too dry, add a bit more water.
5. Divide the masa into 4 equal portions, rolling each into a ball. Using a tortilla press lined with plastic on both sides, press a ball of masa to form a tortilla with a 7-inch diameter.
6. With the tortilla still on the press, remove the top liner and spread 2 heaping tablespoons of the fava bean puree in the center of the tortilla, leaving plenty of room around the circumference.
7. Using the bottom plastic liner, fold the left side onto the middle of the tortilla, then the right, like an envelope. Next, use the liner to nudge the top right side diagonally downward to meet the upper middle, and repeat with the left side. Repeat on the bottom right and left, nudging them diagonally upward to create an oval, or football-shaped, masa pocket to fully encase the filling. Use the top liner to gently smooth out any folds and creases that might occur from the folding. Transfer to a plate. Never done this before? Scan the QR code to see how. Repeat with the remaining masa balls and fava puree, reusing the same plastic liners.
8. Heat a dry comal, griddle, or large skillet over medium heat. Add the tlacoyos seam-side up and cook until the masa is fully cooked and achieves a bit of a char on both sides, 4 to 6 minutes per side.
9. To serve, evenly divide the nopal salsa among the tlacoyos and top with the queso fresco.

Vitamina T(ip)

If you're not able to find nopales that have already been cleaned (stripped of their spines), carefully clean them wearing gloves and using a sharp knife. Set the paddle down on a cutting board and use a knife to cut a thin rim around the edge of the paddle, lift it off, and discard. Slice off the thick bottom end and discard. Then, using a knife or a vegetable peeler, sweep off the remaining spines and their nodes from the surface of each side of the paddle. Wipe the paddle with a paper towel, but do not wash; water activates the slime in the nopal.

Chickpea Tlacoyos with Tahini Crema

MAKES 4 TLACOYOS

- 1 (15-ounce) can chickpeas
- 1 garlic clove, minced
- 3 tablespoons minced cilantro
- 3 tablespoons minced parsley
- ½ cup olive oil
- Juice of 3 lemons (about ½ cup)
- Kosher salt
- ¾ cup tahini
- Grated zest of 2 lemons
- ½ cup ice cold water
- 1½ cups (180g; packed) masa harina, plus more as needed
- Scant 1½ cups (340g) warm (but not hot) water, plus more as needed

Garnishes

- ¾ cup chopped parsley
- 1 tablespoon ground sumac
- Olive oil

Special Equipment

Food processor; tortilla press and plastic liners

How to Make Tlacoyos

There is no such thing as chickpea tlacoyos, to our knowledge—we made them up. Tlacoyos are almost exclusively filled with black beans, favas, or pinto beans, and we simply felt like garbanzos were ready for their close-up in this cross-cultural, Mex-meets-Med remix. While not native to Mexico, garbanzos and sesame seeds are cultivated throughout the country. The chickpea puree is a reference to hummus, and the tahini crema is a nod to tahini sauce.

1. Drain the chickpeas and rinse under running water until the water runs clear. Pick through and discard as many chickpea skins as possible.

2. In a food processor, combine three-fourths of the chickpeas, the garlic, cilantro, and parsley and process for 1 minute. Stop and scrape down the sides of the processor then turn it back on. Slowly stream in the olive oil, followed by the juice of 1 lemon (2 to 3 tablespoons), and process for 2 more minutes to create a smooth, hummus-like texture. Season to taste with salt.

3. In a small bowl, whisk together the tahini, lemon zest, remaining juice of 2 lemons (about ¼ cup), and the ice-cold water until combined. Fold in the reserved whole chickpeas, season to taste with salt, and set aside.

4. Add the masa harina to a medium bowl. Working by hand, mix in the 1½ cups warm water, kneading the dough until the water is fully incorporated and there are no dry spots. It should be moist to the touch but not tacky (leaving bits of wet masa on your hand and fingers). If it's too wet, add a bit more masa harina; if too dry, add a bit more water.

5. Divide the masa into 4 equal portions, rolling each into a ball. Using a tortilla press lined with plastic on both sides, press a ball of masa to form a tortilla with a 7-inch diameter.

6. With the tortilla still on the press, remove the top liner and spread 2 heaping tablespoons of the chickpea puree in the center of the tortilla, leaving plenty of room around the circumference.

7. Using the bottom plastic liner, fold the left side onto the middle of the tortilla, then the right, like an envelope. Next, use the liner to nudge the top right side diagonally downward to meet the upper middle, and repeat with the left side. Repeat on the bottom right and left, nudging them diagonally upward to create an oval, or football-shaped, masa pocket to fully encase the filling. Use the top liner to gently smooth out the folds and creases that might occur from the folding. Transfer to a plate. Never done this before? Scan the QR code to see how. Repeat with the remaining masa balls and chickpea puree, reusing the same plastic liners.

8. Heat a dry comal, griddle, or large skillet over medium heat. Add the tlacoyos seam-side up and cook until the masa is fully cooked and achieves a bit of a char on both sides, 4 to 6 minutes per side.

9. To serve, top each tlacoyo with the tahini-chickpea mixture and garnish each with a sprinkle of the parsley and sumac, then add a drizzle of olive oil.

Picadillo Gorditas

MAKES 5 GORDITAS

1¼ cups (150g; packed) masa harina, plus more as needed

¼ cup (50g) lard or vegetable shortening, at room temperature, plus more for frying

Scant 1¼ cups (285g) warm (but not hot) water, plus more as needed

About 1¼ cups Beef Picadillo (recipe follows)

Garnishes

Shredded iceberg lettuce

Mexican crema

Crumbled queso fresco

½ avocado, sliced

Salsa Roja (page 244)

Special Equipment

Tortilla press and plastic liners (optional)

How to Make Gorditas

As we demonstrated with sopes (see page 194), Mexican food taxonomy can get a bit confusing out there. Gorditas are yet another example of this regionalism as it relates to the naming of things, both within Mexico and beyond. Here, we are specifically cooking up a thicker-set tortilla with a slit down half its circumference, which is then stuffed with picadillo. This is definitely not a recipe for, say, a thick sope or a sweet cake, nor is it a reference to our abuelas' nicknames for our moms, Gordita, or "little chubby one." Oh, and for the record, this gordita is no doubt the inspiration for Taco Bell's Cheesy Gordita Crunch—and yet it's nothing like its fast-food counterpart.

1. Add the masa harina to a large bowl. Working by hand, mix the lard into the masa harina by crumbling it between your fingers. Add the warm water a bit at a time, kneading the dough until the water is fully incorporated, there are no dry spots, and the dough is combined and smooth, 2 to 3 minutes. It should be moist to the touch but not tacky (leaving bits of wet masa on your hand and fingers). If the dough is too wet, add a bit more masa harina; if it's too dry or is cracking, add a bit more water.
2. Divide the dough into 5 equal portions, rolling each into a ball. Using your hands or a tortilla press lined with plastic on both sides, flatten each ball into a thick disk, 3 to 4 inches in diameter and ¼ inch thick, smoothing out any cracks by hand.
3. In a comal or large skillet over medium heat, add a small amount of lard, just enough to lightly coat the bottom of the pan. Add the gorditas and cook until lightly golden and slightly crispy on the outside but still soft on the inside, 2 to 3 minutes on each side. Remove from the skillet and let cool slightly.
4. When cool enough to handle, use a small knife to carefully split the gorditas halfway around the edge, creating a pocket. Never done this before? Scan the QR code to see how.
5. Warm the picadillo if it has cooled. Gently open the pocket of a gordita and spoon 2 to 3 tablespoons of the picadillo into the pocket without overfilling it. Repeat with the remaining gorditas and picadillo.
6. Serve each gordita garnished with the shredded lettuce, crema, queso fresco, sliced avocado, and salsa.

RECIPE CONTINUES →

isha Hot

Beef Picadillo

MAKES 4 CUPS

- 2 dried chipotle chiles
- 1 ancho chile
- Neutral oil
- 1 medium onion, finely diced
- 4 garlic cloves, minced
- 1 pound ground beef
- ½ teaspoon ground cumin
- ½ teaspoon dried Mexican oregano
- ¼ teaspoon ground cinnamon
- ⅛ teaspoon ground allspice
- Kosher salt and freshly ground black pepper
- 2 small potatoes, diced, placed in cold water to prevent browning
- 1 medium carrot, diced
- 3 ripe Roma (plum) tomatoes, chopped

Picadillo is, incidentally, yet another dish that appears in name and varying form throughout parts of Latin America (Puerto Rico, Cuba, Dominican Republic) and even in Asia (Philippines) on account of its Spanish influence. In addition to being a filling for the gorditas here, it is delicious in tacos, quesadillas, or served with rice and beans.

1. In a medium bowl, combine the chipotle and ancho chiles and enough hot water to cover. Soak the chiles for about 20 minutes. Drain the chiles, then remove the stems and seeds, and finely mince.
2. In a large skillet over medium heat, add enough oil to cover the bottom of the pan. When the oil is hot, add the onion and sauté until translucent, about 5 minutes. Add the garlic and sauté until softened, about 3 minutes.
3. Add the ground beef and cook until browned, 1 to 2 minutes, breaking up with a wooden spoon as it cooks. Stir in the minced chiles, the cumin, oregano, cinnamon, allspice, and salt and pepper to taste, and fry until fragrant.
4. Add the potatoes and carrot and cook, stirring occasionally, until the vegetables start to soften, about 5 minutes.
5. Reduce the heat to medium-low, add the tomatoes, and simmer until the tomatoes break down and the vegetables cook through, about 15 minutes. Taste and season with salt and pepper as needed.
6. Transfer the picadillo to an airtight container and store in the fridge for 3 to 5 days until ready to use.

adidas

Puerto Nuevo Lobster Burritos

MAKES 4 BURRITOS

4 small lobster tails (4 to 6 ounces each)

Kosher salt

½ cup (1 stick) unsalted butter

2 teaspoons neutral oil

2 garlic cloves, minced

1 tablespoon minced cilantro

4 Fermín's Flour Tortillas (page 98) or store-bought 6-inch flour tortillas

1 cup Smoky Refried Beans (page 238, made with black beans), warmed

1 cup Arroz a la Mexicana (page 240), warmed

1 cup shredded green cabbage

½ cup Mexican crema (optional)

For Serving

Lime wedges

Pico de Gallo (page 253)

Salsa Roja (page 244)

Buckle up, friends: this lobster burrito is a long way from Qdoba. Hailing from Puerto Nuevo, the "Legendary Lobster Village" located approximately thirty minutes south of San Diego, in Baja California, this burrito is actually not all that geographically far from the nearest Qdoba—but it's anything but the kind you might find at that burrito chain. For starters, there's lobster in it. Additionally, it's more often than not a DIY burrito without the assembly line, where a generous plate of lobster is served with fresh, large flour tortillas, beans, rice, and salsa for your very own custom burrito build.

1. Using kitchen shears, cut the top of each lobster shell lengthwise. Gently pry the shell open and remove the flesh. Discard the shell and season the lobster with salt.
2. In a large skillet over low heat, melt the butter with the oil. Add the garlic and cook until translucent and the butter starts to foam, about 1 minute. Add the lobster and cook through, flipping halfway, about 10 minutes. Remove the pan from the heat, stir in the cilantro, and set aside.
3. To assemble the burritos, spread about ¼ cup of the refried beans in the center of each tortilla, followed by about ¼ cup of the rice. Place a lobster tail on top of the rice. (You can leave the lobster whole for a dramatic look, or cut it into bite-size pieces for easier eating.) Pour some of the lobster-cooking butter over the lobster tail. (Alternatively, serve the butter on the side to dip into.) Add about ¼ cup of the shredded cabbage to each and top with a drizzle of crema (about 2 tablespoons, if using).
4. Roll each tortilla tightly into a burrito, without folding in the sides. Serve with the lime wedges, pico de gallo, and salsa on the side.

ostitos
SABOR
MÁS SALSA VERDE
IMAGEN RELATIVA AL SABOR
IMAGEN RELATIVA AL SABOR

Tostilocos

MAKES 2 GENEROUS SERVINGS

1 (7-ounce) bag Tostitos (the Salsa Verde flavor is a great option)

½ cup cueritos (pickled pork rind)

¼ cup Japanese peanuts

¼ cup grated carrot (about 1 large)

¼ cup grated jicama (about ½ small)

¼ cup grated cucumber (about 1 large)

¼ cup Valentina hot sauce

¼ cup Chamoy, homemade (page 257) or store-bought

2 limes, halved

Tajín

2 banderillas de tamarindo (tamarind candy straws; optional)

This after-school delicacy is not for the faint of heart. Tostilocos is the kind of dish that happens when a Mexican fruit-vendor-turned-mobile-corner-store puts all of its inventory together at the request of an elementary school student with a couple of extra pesos to spare. And, if you were to really channel your inner child—you know, the one who had yet to be hardened by soul-sucking adult things like utility bills, online dating, and wellness podcasts on the ills of our modern industrialized diet—you'd see for yourself just how tostilocos, and its cousin, dorilocos, managed to not only catch on in mainstream Mexican culture but also endure as one of the most legendary vitamina T staples of all time.

1 Place the Tostitos bag on its side and, using scissors, cut a horizontal opening. Top the Tostitos with the cueritos, peanuts, and grated vegetables. Hold the bag closed and shake to mix everything as much as possible without breaking the chips.

2 Reopen the bag and drizzle the hot sauce and chamoy over the top of the chip mixture. Squeeze lime on top and sprinkle on as much Tajín as you want. Garnish with a tamarind candy straw, if desired, and share with someone you don't mind swapping germs with. Or just go all in yourself, but don't blame us for the tummy ache.

The Golden

Enchiladas Verdes

SERVES 2

- 1½ pounds boneless, skinless chicken breasts
- 1 cup roughly diced celery (about 2 medium stalks)
- 1 medium onion, coarsely diced
- 1 head of garlic, halved horizontally
- 1 bay leaf
- Kosher salt
- 2 cups Salsa Verde (page 245)
- 1 cup Mexican crema, plus more for garnish
- ½ cup heavy cream
- 3 tablespoons neutral oil, plus more as needed
- 6 corn tortillas, homemade (page 97) or store-bought
- 1 cup (loosely packed) hand-pulled strands quesillo (a.k.a. queso Oaxaca), or ¾ cup shredded low-moisture mozzarella
- Minced cilantro, for garnish

Special Equipment

Blender; instant-read digital thermometer (optional)

This is one of those classic crowd-pleasing dishes that we just had to slide in here, even if it didn't exactly conform to the initial premise of this cookbook. (FWIW, we *have* encountered at least one vendor in Mexico selling enchiladas from the trunk of his car, but not quite like these.) Enchiladas hardly need any introduction at all; they are, in fact, right up there with tacos and tamales as some of the most heavily sought-after recipes on the internet. If this is somehow your first time encountering them, think of baked enchiladas as a tortilla casserole with generous amounts of salsa, cheese, and protein—often chicken, as is the case here. This recipe is of the green variety, which comes from the tomatillos, and is of the suiza (i.e., enchiladas suizas, or Swiss enchiladas) persuasion, on account of having cream mixed into the salsa.

1. In a medium soup pot, combine the chicken, celery, onion, garlic, and bay leaf and add water to cover by 2 inches. Generously salt the water and bring to a boil over medium-high heat, then reduce the heat to bring to a simmer, making sure to skim and discard any impurities that rise to the surface. Simmer until the chicken is cooked through and tender, 20 to 25 minutes.
2. Meanwhile, in a blender, combine the salsa, crema, and heavy cream and blend until uniform. Season to taste with salt.
3. Remove the chicken from the pot and place in a bowl to cool. (Reserve the chicken stock for future use. Strain into an airtight container and store in the fridge for 5 to 7 days or in the freezer for 2 to 3 months.)
4. When the chicken is cool enough to handle, use clean hands or 2 forks to shred it as finely as possible. Season with about 2 teaspoons of salt or to taste.
5. Preheat the oven to 350°F and lightly oil an 8 × 8 × 2-inch baking dish.
6. In a large skillet over medium heat, warm the oil. Line a plate with paper towels and keep near the stove. Lightly fry the tortillas one at a time until lightly golden, about 15 seconds per side, and set them on the paper towels to drain, covering them with a clean kitchen towel to keep them warm as they come off the skillet. (This step will help make sure the tortillas don't break as you are rolling them into enchiladas.)
7. Fill each tortilla with some chicken and roll it up into a cigar shape. Place the rolls seam-side down in the prepared baking dish.
8. Pour the sauce over the enchiladas, and top with the quesillo. Bake the enchiladas until the cheese on top has melted and the chicken in the enchiladas is warm in the center, about 25 minutes. (Test the chicken by inserting a toothpick or an instant-read digital thermometer into the center of the enchilada; if the toothpick comes out warm, the chicken is ready.)
9. Serve garnished with additional crema and the cilantro.

Chilaquiles Verdes

SERVES 2

- 1 tablespoon olive oil
- 2 large eggs
- Kosher salt and freshly ground black pepper
- 1½ to 2½ cups Salsa Verde (page 245)
- 6 ounces (4 cups) totopos (see Tip) or store-bought tortilla chips

Garnishes

- ½ medium red onion, thinly sliced
- ¼ cup Mexican crema
- Cilantro leaves
- ½ cup grated Cotija cheese

As you might have already concluded from our note on the Chilaquiles Torta (page 66), as well as this photo, we find chilaquiles and Electrolit to be a stellar cure for a hangover. But while feeling crudo can sometimes help us justify eating tortilla chips—a.k.a. totopos (ahem, vitamina T)—and salsa for breakfast, chilaquiles are by no means solely limited to this occasion. When it comes to their finished texture, we are partial to crunchy-soggy, not soggy-soggy. Be sure to taste the chips as they're simmering in the salsa in order to dial into your desired bite.

1. In a medium skillet over medium heat, warm the olive oil. Crack in the eggs, and season with salt and pepper. Cook until the whites are set, then carefully transfer to a plate.
2. In a large saucepan over medium-low heat, warm 1½ cups of the salsa verde. Toss in the chips and stir to generously coat. There should be more salsa than needed to coat the chips—if not, add more salsa as needed. Remove from the heat and season to taste with salt.
3. Spoon half the chilaquiles onto each plate, top each with a fried egg, and garnish each with half the onion, 2 tablespoons of the crema, cilantro, and half the cheese.

Vitamina T(ip)

To make the totopos, cut 6 corn tortillas into triangles with a sharp knife. (Dry or stale corn tortillas work best.) You can cut them into fourths or eighths, depending on the size of chip you want. In a large, deep skillet over medium-high heat, warm about 2 inches of neutral oil. Test the heat by dropping a piece of tortilla into the oil to be sure it sizzles. Working in batches and using tongs, add the tortilla triangles one by one to the pan in a single layer. Fry until golden and crispy, 1 to 2 minutes per side, adding more oil as needed. Remove from the pan and place onto a paper towel–lined plate. Season with salt while hot, and continue to fry the remaining triangles.

Electrolit
ELECTROLYTE BEVERAGE
Premium Hydration
Grape

Fruit with Tajín and Chamoy

SERVES 4

- 2 cups fresh pineapple chunks (about ½ medium)
- 2 cups roughly diced watermelon (about ¼ medium)
- 2 cups roughly diced peeled jicama
- 1 Honeycrisp apple, cored and cut into large dice
- Juice of 2 limes
- 1 teaspoon Morton kosher salt
- Chamoy, homemade (page 257) or store-bought
- Tajín or Aleppo pepper

We really did include a recipe for cut fruit and store-bought Tajín because it's just that iconic—plus, we felt compelled to work a homemade chamoy (a sweet-sour-spicy Mexican condiment) into the conversation. Mangoes are notably absent from this dish, as they always seem to hog the limelight, but that shouldn't stop you from including any combination of fruits (+ jicama) that you desire. Fruit cart optional!

1. In a large bowl, combine the pineapple, watermelon, jicama, and apple. Add the lime juice and sprinkle with the salt.
2. Place the fruit in individual bowls or keep in the large bowl for serving. Lightly drizzle the top with chamoy and sprinkle with as much Tajín as you want!

Vanilla Conchas

MAKES 12 CONCHAS

Topping Rounds

¾ cup (90g) all-purpose flour

¾ cup (90g) confectioners' sugar

½ cup (100g) vegetable shortening

1½ teaspoons vanilla extract

Dough

1½ teaspoons active dry yeast

1 cup (240g) warm (but not hot) whole milk

4 cups (500g) all-purpose flour, plus more as needed

1 teaspoon Morton kosher salt

3 large eggs

1 teaspoon vanilla extract

½ cup (95g) granulated sugar

5 tablespoons (70g) unsalted butter, at room temperature, cut into 1-inch cubes

2 tablespoons vegetable shortening

Neutral oil

Special Equipment

Stand mixer; digital scale; tortilla press and plastic liners; concha cutter/stamp (optional)

Conchas are a Mexican breakfast staple typically enjoyed with a sidecar of Champurrado (page 177) or coffee for dunking. They are close to brioche buns in texture and are enveloped with a striated, sweet and crunchy topping that, once baked, gives the pastry a concha, or shell-like, appearance, hence their name. Like most fresh breads out there, the difference between a great concha and a not-so-good concha is when you eat it. They really are best enjoyed the moment they're out of the oven, but if you want to get extra, you can always split them in half and stuff with any number of fillings, as in the Concha with Nata (page 86).

1. **Make the topping rounds:** In a stand mixer fitted with the paddle attachment, mix the flour and confectioners' sugar on low speed (setting 2 on a KitchenAid) until well combined. Add the shortening and mix on low speed until combined, then, with the mixer still running, stream in the vanilla.
2. Remove the topping mixture from the mixer bowl and divide it into 12 equal portions (about 25g each). Roll each portion into a ball, place on a plate, and allow to firm up in the fridge for 15 minutes.
3. Using a tortilla press lined with plastic on both sides, lightly press each ball to form a thick round about 4½ inches in diameter. Remove the round from the plastic and carefully layer it between 2 pieces of parchment paper. Repeat with the remaining balls. Place in the fridge to chill until you're ready to make the conchas, taking care not to compress them.
4. **Make the dough:** In a small bowl, mix the yeast into the warmed milk and let stand until bubbles form, about 10 minutes. Meanwhile, clean the bowl of the mixer and switch to the dough hook attachment. Add the flour along with the salt and mix at low speed (setting 2) to combine. With the mixer still running, slowly incorporate the yeast-milk mixture.
5. When the milk mixture is fully incorporated, crack in one egg at a time and mix on medium-low speed (setting 4), beating well after each addition. You're looking for a dough that is smooth and creamy, so if it looks at all lumpy, keep the machine going before adding the next egg. With the mixer still running, stream in the vanilla.

6. Incorporate the granulated sugar and butter in 3 alternating batches, making sure each ingredient is fully incorporated before adding the next. The dough will start to come together and should easily pull from the sides as it's mixing. When all the sugar and butter are incorporated, if your dough is not pulling away from the bowl, add up to 3 tablespoons of flour, 1 tablespoon at a time, until the dough comes together. Finally, add the shortening and mix until fully incorporated.

7. Lightly oil the inside of a large bowl. Transfer the dough to the bowl, cover with a clean kitchen towel or plastic wrap, and let rest at room temperature until the dough doubles in size, 1 to 1½ hours, depending on your kitchen temperature.

8. Lightly flour a work surface. Punch down the dough, divide into 12 equal portions (about 90g each), and shape into balls. Line 2 sheet pans with parchment paper, then transfer the balls to the pans, making sure to leave about 3 inches between the balls to allow them to expand. Cover each of the pans with a light towel and let rest at room temperature for 10 minutes.

9. Remove the towels from the sheet pans and remove the topping rounds from the fridge. Place one round on top of each ball of dough. If you're using a concha cutter, lightly press it into the topping to make the signature shell design.

10. Allow the conchas to rest, uncovered, until they have expanded by about one-third, 15 to 20 minutes. Preheat the oven to 350°F.

11. Bake the conchas for 15 to 18 minutes, or until they have doubled in size and are firm on the outside and the topping has hardened. Transfer to a wire rack to rest for 5 minutes before eating.

Churros

MAKES 8 TO 12 CHURROS

Dough

½ cup (125g) milk

5 tablespoons (70g) unsalted butter

2 tablespoons sugar

1 teaspoon vanilla extract

½ teaspoon Morton kosher salt

1 cup (120g) all-purpose flour

2 large eggs

To Finish

2 cups sugar

4½ teaspoons ground cinnamon

Neutral oil, for frying

Special Equipment

Stand mixer (optional); piping bag with large open star tip (#824, #825, or #826); candy/deep-fry thermometer (optional)

We are calling churros an honorary staple of the vitamina T familia, despite the fact that they are not native to Mexico—they're Spanish and Portuguese in origin with, some believe, even earlier ties to China—nor do they start with the letter *T*. Consider doubling the dough recipe and saving a batch in your freezer, as churros are rather prep-intensive.

1. In a wide saucepan, combine ½ cup of water, the milk, butter, sugar, vanilla, and salt and bring to a boil over medium-high heat.
2. Turn off the heat and add the flour. Set the pan over medium heat and mix vigorously using a wooden spoon until the ingredients are fully combined and the dough pulls away from the sides of the pan.
3. Transfer the dough to the bowl of a stand mixer and cover with plastic wrap. Let sit for 5 minutes to cool. (If the dough is too hot when you add the eggs, you run the risk of scrambling them.)
4. With the paddle or dough hook attachment, mix the dough on medium speed (setting 5 or 6 on a KitchenAid), adding the eggs one at a time and allowing each egg to be fully incorporated before adding the next. The dough may break at various points but it will come back together as you mix. (Alternatively, mix in the eggs by hand, but it's important the dough is not too hot.)
5. Turn out the dough onto plastic wrap and wrap it up. Refrigerate it until it firms up to the consistency of tortilla dough, 2 to 3 hours. The firmer the dough, the more tubular your churros and the more distinct the ridges will be.
6. Once firm, remove the dough from the fridge and transfer to a piping bag fitted with an open star tip, making sure to squeeze out any air pockets in the piping bag (see Tip).
7. In a shallow bowl at least 7 inches wide, mix the sugar and cinnamon.
8. In a large, deep pot, add enough oil to come halfway up the sides and clip a candy/deep-fry thermometer to the inside of the pot. Heat the oil over medium-high heat until the temperature reaches 375°F. (If you don't have a thermometer, dip the handle of a wooden spoon into the oil. If the oil bubbles vigorously around the handle, it's hot enough.) Set a wire rack in a sheet pan and keep near the stove.
9. Holding the piping bag a few inches above the hot oil, carefully pipe out the churros. Using kitchen scissors, cut off the piping every 6 inches or so. (Alternatively, pipe the churros onto parchment in 6-inch logs, wrap them, and freeze for up to 1 month, or until ready to cook.) Working in batches to avoid overcrowding and allowing the oil to come back to temperature after each batch, fry the churros until golden brown, 5 to 6 minutes. If there's not enough room for them to fully submerge in the oil, flip them halfway through to ensure contact with the hot oil. Remove the cooked churros from the oil as they are done and drain them on the wire rack for 30 to 60 seconds. Roll the hot churros in the cinnamon sugar and enjoy immediately.

Vitamina T(ip)
The size of the piping tip will determine how quickly the churros cook. It's important to look for a star tip (to maintain the churros' ridges) with an opening of between ½ and ¾ inch. An opening of more than ¾ inch may create steam pockets in the dough, which can pop in the oil and cause splashback.

Buñuelos with Cinnamon Sugar

MAKES 12 BUÑUELOS

1¼ cups (310g) whole milk

2 tablespoons unsalted butter

Neutral oil

3⅓ cups (425g) all-purpose flour, plus more for dusting

2 teaspoons baking powder

2 teaspoons Morton kosher salt

2 cups (400g) sugar

1½ tablespoons ground cinnamon

Special Equipment

Digital scale; candy/deep-fry thermometer (optional)

We can't stop you from the quick hack of frying flour tortillas—especially the uncooked packaged flour tortillas that some markets sell—and calling them buñuelos. That method works: It produces a result that is technically still a fritter (i.e., a buñuelo) and has fooled our extended families on more than one holiday occasion. But if you have the time and you're feeling a little more peace and/or a lot less anxiety toward your family this upcoming Christmas, consider going the extra forty-five minutes to show—not just tell—that you really love them.

1. In a small saucepan over medium-low heat, combine the milk, butter, and 2½ tablespoons of oil and warm until the butter is melted and the mixture is warm to the touch. Do not allow the milk to boil or scald.
2. In a large bowl, combine the flour, baking powder, and salt. Make a well in the center of the dry mixture, then pour the warmed milk mixture into the well. Using a rubber spatula and/or your hands, fold the dry ingredients into the wet ingredients until just combined (you may need to knead by hand for 2 to 3 minutes). The dough should look shaggy and feel tacky to the touch but not sticky. Be careful not to overwork the dough, as it will yield a tough tortilla.
3. Lightly oil the inside of another large bowl and place the ball of dough inside. Cover the bowl with plastic wrap and let rest in the fridge for 30 minutes.
4. Remove the bowl from the fridge. Divide the dough into 12 equal portions (about 65g each) and roll into balls. Place the dough balls on a plate or sheet pan and cover with a damp towel. Let rest for 15 minutes.
5. In a shallow bowl at least 7 inches wide, mix the sugar and cinnamon, then set aside.
6. Lightly flour a work surface and roll out each ball of dough into a tortilla about ⅛ inch thick and roughly 4 to 5 inches in diameter.
7. Pour 2 inches of oil into a Dutch oven or wide, heavy pot and clip a candy/deep-fry thermometer to the inside of the pot. Heat the oil over medium heat until the temperature reaches 350°F. (If you don't have a thermometer, dip the handle of a wooden spoon into the oil. If the oil bubbles around the handle, it's hot enough.) Set a wire rack in a sheet pan.
8. Using a slotted spoon or spider strainer, carefully place a round of dough in the hot oil. As soon as the dough begins to puff, flip it over to prevent it from puffing further. Continue flipping and frying until both sides are golden brown, 2 to 3 minutes total.
9. Place the buñuelos on the rack to drain and cool slightly, 30 to 60 seconds. Then dredge each side of the buñuelos in the cinnamon sugar. Repeat for the remaining rounds of dough, allowing the oil to come back to temperature, frying the dough and then draining and dredging with the cinnamon sugar. Enjoy immediately.

TOQUES
FINALES

Final touches

“T” is for team, and vitamina T is a team sport, friends. Last time we checked, there is no “I” in suadero; so just because final touches appear later in the game doesn’t make them any less important than the main dishes themselves. Shohei Ohtani may indeed have been the center of attention in 2024, but let’s not forget that Freddie Freeman would eventually go on to hit the first walk-off grand slam in World Series history at the bottom of the tenth. That’s some game-winning sazón right there. Go Dodgers.

Speaking of sazón, the following recipes are full of it. These are the supporting players that have the power to bring just about any vitamina T dish to life. In fact, there is a paradoxical saying in Mexico that goes, “Un taco sin salsa no es taco” (A taco without salsa isn’t a taco), which should give you a taste of just how critical condiments are to Mexico’s street food culture. Of course, any mound of food atop a soft tortilla can technically be considered a taco, but that’s beside the point. As Dani Rojas might say off the pitch, accoutrements are life, and we couldn’t agree more.

As far as how and when to use condiments, that is ultimately up to you. Throughout this cookbook, we have noted pairings we like on particular dishes, but that doesn’t stop us from applying additional garnishes and condiments, like cilantro and onion, refried beans, lime, and salsas (plural), to these dishes and beyond—and it shouldn’t stop you either.

So go forth and sprinkle that Chorizo Rojo (page 237) into your next bowl of pasta al pomodoro, dip that chip right into those Charro Beans (page 239), and spread some Salsa Macha (page 252) onto that turkey club sandwich. We’ll be right here for every last drop of it.

Chorizo Rojo

MAKES 2 POUNDS (3½ CUPS)

- 5 guajillo chiles, stemmed, seeded, and veins removed
- 3 dried puya (pulla) chiles, stemmed, seeded, and veins removed
- ½ medium onion, roughly diced
- 2 garlic cloves, peeled
- ½ cup apple cider vinegar
- 1½ teaspoons dried Mexican oregano
- 1½ tablespoons Morton kosher salt, plus more as needed
- ½ cinnamon stick (preferably Mexican canela)
- 2½ pounds ground pork
- 2 tablespoons neutral oil

Special Equipment

Blender (preferably high-powered, such as Vitamix)

They say no one wants to know how the sausage is made, but this chorizo rojo really isn't that kind of sausage. There will be no mystery meat, vinegary casings, or pink salts to speak of—just some ground pork, chiles, and aromatics blended and rendered to crumbly perfection. In addition to boasting a fresher ingredient list than most store-bought chorizos, this homemade recipe invites you to dial in your salt and spice levels according to personal preference. Feel free to experiment with different chile combinations, too, if you're feeling adventurous.

1. In a medium saucepan, combine the guajillo and puya chiles, onion, garlic, vinegar, oregano, salt, and cinnamon stick. Add just enough water to cover the ingredients. Bring to a boil over medium-high heat, then reduce to a simmer and cook until the onion, garlic, and chiles are soft, about 45 minutes, using tongs to test consistency. Let cool slightly. Drain the mixture in a strainer, reserving the cooking liquid. If you aren't using a high-powered blender, remove the cinnamon stick.
2. Add the cooked mixture to a blender along with about 2 cups of the cooking liquid and blend to make a smooth puree.
3. In a medium metal bowl, season the pork lightly with salt and mix in the puree. (If cooking the chorizo for another recipe that includes potatoes, as in Tacos de Canasta on page 140, or Chorizo and Potato Pambazo on page 70, stop here and proceed according to that recipe's instructions.)
4. In a large skillet over medium heat, warm the oil. Add the pork mixture and sauté, breaking up the pork every few minutes with a spatula, until it is cooked through, 10 to 15 minutes. It should be deep red in color and crumbly in texture. Season to taste with salt. Cooked chorizo can be stored in an airtight container in the fridge for 3 to 5 days.

Smoky Refried Beans

MAKES 5 TO 6 CUPS

- 1 cup dried black or pinto beans, soaked for 6 to 12 hours (see Tip)
- 6 garlic cloves, peeled
- 1 medium onion, quartered
- 5 dried epazote sprigs
- 2 chipotle chiles, stemmed and seeded
- 5 cascabel chiles, stemmed and seeded
- 1 dried avocado leaf
- 1 teaspoon dried Mexican oregano
- 1 teaspoon cumin seeds
- 1½ tablespoons white wine vinegar, rice vinegar, or sherry vinegar (optional)
- ¼ cup lard or refined coconut oil
- Kosher salt

Special Equipment

- Blender

We promise that we are proponents of the less-is-more approach when it comes to cooking, especially refried beans, but we just couldn't help ourselves from working in some chiles and vinegar for the sake of balance. Refried beans are, well, fried in lard, which makes them richer than standard-issue braised beans, so the added acidity and mild spice were summoned to even out the decadence a bit. You'll still find all the usual aromatics, including peppery epazote (a homeopathic gas reliever, BTW) and dried avocado leaf for a kiss of anise-y sweetness.

1. In a 6-quart pot, combine the beans, garlic, onion, epazote, chipotle chiles, cascabel chiles, avocado leaf, oregano, and cumin. Add enough water to cover the beans by 5 inches and bring to a rolling boil over high heat. Reduce the heat to medium and cook until the beans are tender, 1 to 3 hours, adding more water as needed if they look dry. (The cook time will vary depending on the age of the beans and whether they were soaked; see Tip.)
2. When the beans are cooked, discard the epazote and avocado leaf. Drain the bean mixture in a strainer, reserving the cooking liquid. Working in batches to avoid overfilling the blender, add the cooked ingredients, along with 1 cup of the bean-cooking liquid, and blend until smooth. Add additional cooking liquid as needed to create a smooth texture, like thick potato soup. Stir in the vinegar (if using).
3. In a 6-quart pot over high heat, warm the lard. When hot and melted, carefully pour the bean puree into the pot. Reduce the heat to medium-low and cook, whisking occasionally to avoid burning the bottom of the pot, until the beans are warmed through and the lard is fully incorporated, 5 to 10 minutes. Don't rush this step: You want the mixture to fully emulsify. Remove the pot from the heat and season to taste with salt. Store in an airtight container in the fridge for 5 to 7 days, or in the freezer for up to 2 months.

Vitamina T(ip)

If you forget to soak your beans ahead of time, don't worry! Just increase the cooking time.

Charro Beans

MAKES 3½ CUPS

- 2 slices bacon, cut into ½-inch pieces
- ¼ small onion, finely diced
- 2 garlic cloves, minced
- 1 jalapeño chile, stemmed and sliced into rounds
- 1 teaspoon ground cumin
- 1 medium ripe tomato, finely diced
- 1 cup dried pinto or bayo beans
- 3 cups beef or chicken stock (preferably low-sodium)
- Kosher salt

A charro is the Mexican equivalent of a cowboy, which means that these are cowboy beans. What exactly makes them cowboy beans? If you, like the unknown progenitor of this dish, subscribe to stereotypes about cowboys, you might say that bacon, pinto beans, and cumin are on-the-border cowboyish. They'd be really cowboyish if you were to cook them over an open fire, out on the mesa, under a heavy blanket of stars . . . nothing but you, your horse, and your sombrero doing everyday cowboy things, like making these here cowboy beans. Giddyup.

1. Heat a large saucepan over medium heat and add the bacon. When the bacon starts to release its fat, add the onion, garlic, jalapeño, and cumin. Cook until the vegetables soften, 2 to 4 minutes.
2. Add the diced tomato, stirring constantly to break it down and combine with the rest of the ingredients, 1 to 2 minutes.
3. Add the beans and stock and increase the heat to bring to a boil. Reduce the heat to medium-low, cover, and cook at a low simmer until the beans are tender, 1 to 3 hours, testing for tenderness every 30 minutes. Season to taste with salt.

Arroz a la Mexicana

MAKES 2 CUPS

3 guajillo chiles, stemmed, seeded, and veins removed

2 cups chicken stock (preferably low-sodium)

Neutral oil

1 cup long-grain white rice

½ cup finely diced onion (about ¼ onion)

1 garlic clove, minced

1 teaspoon Morton kosher salt, plus more as needed

Special Equipment

Blender

This recipe for arroz a la Mexicana, or Mexican rice, is not your traditional tomato-infused rice studded with cubed carrots, peas, and the occasional sweet corn kernels. In fact, we're not sure that you'll even feel comfortable with us calling this arroz a la Mexicana after all we've done to it, but we have no regrets. Standing in for tomatoes are guajillo chiles, which maintain this classic's dark orange color and baseline tanginess while adding a touch of warmth. There will be no vegetable garnishes that remind us of our middle-school cafeteria food, just the good stuff. Also, let's not forget that guajillos are native to Mexico, after all, and perhaps this rice is just as Mexican, if not more so, than its original counterpart.

1. In a medium bowl, combine the guajillo chiles and enough hot water to cover. Soak the guajillos until soft, about 5 minutes. Drain and add to a blender along with the chicken stock. Blend until smooth and set aside.
2. In a medium skillet over medium heat, warm enough oil to lightly coat the bottom of the pan. Add the rice and toast until golden brown, stirring constantly so it doesn't burn.
3. Add the onion and garlic and cook until they appear translucent. Add the chile puree and bring the mixture to a boil. While the mixture comes to a boil, add the salt, taste the liquid and add more salt as needed.
4. Reduce the heat to low, cover, and cook until all the liquid has been absorbed and the grains are tender, about 15 minutes. Turn off the heat and let rest, covered, for 10 minutes.
5. Fluff the rice with a fork before serving.

11
12
10
13
9
8

1 Salsa Verde Cruda (page 249)
2 Salsa de Chile de Árbol (page 250)
3 Pico de Gallo (page 253)
4 Salsa Morita (page 248)
5 Salsa Tatemada (page 247)
6 Guacamole (page 255)
7 Chipotle Mayo (page 253)
8 Salsa Macha (page 252)
9 Salsa Verde (page 245)
10 Salsa Taquera (page 246)
11 Salsa Roja (page 244)
12 Salsa de Molcajete (page 251)
13 Salsa Morita with Chicharrón (page 248)

Salsa Roja

MAKES 3 TO 4 CUPS

- 4 guajillo chiles, stemmed, seeded, and veins removed
- 2 chiles de árbol, stemmed and seeded
- 3 ripe Roma (plum) tomatoes, halved
- ½ medium onion, quartered
- 5 garlic cloves, peeled
- ¾ teaspoon cumin seeds or ground cumin
- ½ bunch of cilantro, roughly chopped (leaves and tender stems; about 1 cup)
- Juice of 1 lime
- Kosher salt

Special Equipment

Blender or food processor; spice grinder or molcajete (if using cumin seeds)

Salsa roja is a taqueria's obligatory red salsa that will often appear alongside avocado salsa (see Salsa Taquera, page 246). In contrast to the creamy avocado salsa, salsa roja is a bit less viscous, especially when made with a blender, like most taquerias do. Because of the charred red chiles, salsa roja is also notably more bitter than its green counterpart, which is brighter and more acidic. This version is quite mild, making it a great choice for the spice-averse. All this being said, roja and verde are excellent companions both on and off their condiment caddies, combined in any taco of your choice.

1. Heat a comal, griddle, or large skillet over medium heat. Toast the guajillo and árbol chiles until fragrant but not burnt. Remove the chiles from the pan.
2. In a medium pot, bring about 5 cups of water to a boil. Add the toasted chiles, the tomatoes, onion, and garlic. Reduce the heat and simmer until the tomatoes are soft and the chiles are rehydrated, 12 to 15 minutes.
3. If using cumin seeds, while the ingredients are simmering, toast the seeds in a dry pan over medium heat until fragrant, about 30 seconds. Grind to a powder using a spice grinder or molcajete.
4. Reserving ½ cup of their cooking liquid, drain the cooked ingredients and transfer to a blender or food processor. Add the cumin and cilantro, then blend, streaming in ¼ cup of the reserved cooking liquid and adding more liquid as needed to achieve a smooth texture.
5. Add the lime juice and season to taste with salt. Store in an airtight container in the fridge for 5 to 7 days.

Salsa Verde

MAKES 3 TO 4 CUPS

- 1 tablespoon and 1 teaspoon Morton kosher salt, plus more as needed
- 10 medium tomatillos, husked and rinsed
- ½ medium onion, quartered
- 3 garlic cloves, peeled
- 2 jalapeño chiles, stemmed (seeded if you prefer a milder salsa)
- ½ cup minced cilantro (leaves and tender stems)
- Juice of 1 lime, plus more as needed

Special Equipment

Blender

This boiled tomatillo salsa verde is our go-to for Chilaquiles Verdes (page 222), but it's also perfect on Carnitas Tacos (page 106), burritos, most tamales, and whatever else you feel compelled to put it on. Think acid-forward with a subtle hit of umami and a medium dose of green heat.

1. In a medium pot over high heat, bring about 5 cups of water and 1 tablespoon of salt to a boil.
2. Carefully add the tomatillos, onion, garlic, and jalapeños. Reduce the heat to medium and simmer until the tomatillos turn pale and the onion is tender, 7 to 8 minutes. Reserving ½ cup of the cooking liquid, drain and let cool for 5 minutes.
3. In a blender, combine the cooked vegetables, the reserved cooking liquid, the cilantro, lime juice, and 1 teaspoon of salt. Pulse at low speed until you achieve a lightly blended sauce that still has some texture to it. If the salsa is too thick, add 2 tablespoons of water at a time, until the desired consistency is reached. Taste and season with more salt or lime juice as needed.
4. Transfer to a bowl and let cool to room temperature. Store in an airtight container in the fridge for 5 to 7 days.

Salsa Taquera

MAKES ABOUT 4 CUPS

- 1 tablespoon Morton kosher salt, plus more as needed
- 4 medium-large tomatillos, husked, rinsed, and halved
- 1 small zucchini, cut into 1-inch-thick rounds
- 3 garlic cloves, peeled
- 3 tablespoons neutral oil
- 2 jalapeño chiles, stemmed and halved lengthwise
- 1 bunch of cilantro
- 1 avocado, halved

Special Equipment

Blender

Salsa de aguacate, or avocado salsa, has the hat-trick quality of being acidic, spicy, and cooling all at the same time. While some versions of this light green, creamy salsa feature raw tomatillos, we prefer them boiled to mellow their pectin and soften the salsa to a silken texture. Most taquerias offer a self-serve version of this miracle condiment—a bold business move when you consider the average price of avocados and that a certain fast-food burrito chain charges nearly three dollars for a small side of basic guac. But there's often a hidden ingredient folded into this selfless service detail: zucchini. Taqueros have cleverly relied on this vegetable as a value-driven, viridescent thickener in the name of excellent salsa hospitality, and we salute them for it.

1. In a medium pot, combine 5 cups of water with the salt and bring to a boil over high heat. Once the water is boiling, carefully add the tomatillos, zucchini, and garlic. Reduce the heat to medium and simmer until the tomatillos turn army green and the zucchini is tender when pierced with a fork, 7 to 10 minutes. Drain and set aside to cool slightly.
2. In a small skillet over medium heat, warm the oil. Once hot, add the jalapeños and fry until they become fragrant and slightly crisp, about 3 minutes on each side, checking every minute or so to be careful not to burn them. Remove the chiles and set aside to cool slightly, reserving the oil.
3. In a blender, combine the tomatillo mixture, the jalapeños, reserved cooking oil, and the cilantro. Scoop in the avocado flesh. Blend, starting at low speed and gradually increasing to high, until it is smooth and uniform. Add water as needed to reach a loose, pourable consistency.
4. Season to taste with salt. Store in an airtight container in the fridge for 5 to 7 days.

Salsa Tatemada

MAKES ABOUT 3 CUPS

- 5 piquín chiles
- 3 ripe Roma (plum) tomatoes, halved
- 1 medium white onion, ½ quartered and ½ finely diced
- 5 garlic cloves, unpeeled
- 4 Fresno chiles, stemmed, halved lengthwise, and seeded (jalapeños make a good, if less spicy, substitute)
- ½ bunch of cilantro, chopped (leaves and tender stems; about 1 cup)
- Kosher salt

Special Equipment

Molcajete or food processor

How to Use a Molcajete

Tatemada means "burnt" or "blistered," and there are multiple ways to tatemar these salsa ingredients to get the job done. We have called for the traditional stovetop comal approach, but the broiler method, for instance, will also do the trick. Between the piquín chiles (tiny but fiery) and the Fresno chiles (spicy like a jalapeño while fruity like a bell pepper), this is a spicier salsa tatemada than we're used to seeing, with some uncharacteristic raw ingredients added. Incidentally, it is also fairly unconventional for the Fresno, a U.S.-bred chile developed in the 1950s, to make a salsa cameo, but we felt that it deserved some playing time. Feel free to tone down the heat by either reducing the chile count to your preference or swapping jalapeños for the Fresnos.

1. Heat a comal, griddle, or large skillet over medium heat. Toast the piquín chiles for about 30 seconds per side, until fragrant but not burnt. (You may want to open a window, as the capsaicin—the spicy component from the chiles—will release into the air.) Set aside.
2. In the same comal, separately char the tomatoes, the quartered onion, garlic, and Fresno chiles, turning occasionally, until lightly charred on all sides, about 10 minutes. Remove from the heat. Once cool, peel the garlic.
3. Using the tejolote (pestle) of your molcajete, grind the toasted piquín chiles to a powder. Add the charred onion, garlic, and Fresnos, and mash until well incorporated. Finish with the charred tomatoes, grinding until you get a rustic, chunky texture. Not familiar with using a molcajete? Scan the QR code for a visual. (Alternatively, use a food processor. Combine the toasted chiles with the other ingredients and pulse in short bursts to achieve a chunky texture, adding water as needed.)
4. Fold in the diced onion and cilantro then serve right in the molcajete or transfer the salsa to a bowl. Season to taste with salt. Store in an airtight container in the fridge for 5 to 7 days.

Salsa Morita

MAKES ABOUT 2 CUPS

- 1 tablespoon Morton kosher salt, plus more as needed
- 5 medium tomatillos, husked, rinsed, and halved
- ½ medium onion, quartered
- 5 garlic cloves, peeled
- 4 morita chiles, stemmed and seeded
- 2 tablespoons annatto seeds, or 1 tablespoon achiote paste
- ½ bunch of cilantro, roughly chopped (leaves and tender stems; about 1 cup)
- Kosher salt

Special Equipment

- Blender

Walking into a taqueria for the very first time, Fermín knows he's in for a good taco when he encounters one or all of the following details: (1) hanging bags of Marli brand napkins, (2) a sign that says "pago solo en efectivo" (cash only), and/or (3) a salsa morita stationed near the customary Salsa Taquera (page 246). With respect to the salsa, morita chiles are relatively less common in the wild and also a bit more expensive to the operator, so their very appearance expresses a certain quality of care and quiet luxury.

1. In a medium pot over high heat, bring about 5 cups of water and the salt to a boil. Carefully add the tomatillos, onion, garlic, and morita chiles. If using annatto seeds, add them now; if using achiote paste, reserve for later. Reduce the heat to medium and simmer until the tomatillos turn pale and the onion is tender, 10 to 12 minutes. Drain the cooked ingredients, reserving ½ cup of the cooking liquid, and let cool for 5 minutes.
2. In a blender, combine the cooked ingredients, the reserved cooking liquid, and the cilantro. If using achiote paste instead of annatto seeds, add it now. Blend on low speed for 30 seconds, then gradually increase to high. Blend until smooth, 1 to 2 minutes, ensuring the annatto seeds (if using) are finely ground.
3. Taste and season with salt as needed, starting with 1 tablespoon, then pour the salsa into a bowl. Let the salsa cool to room temperature before serving. Store in an airtight container in the fridge for 5 to 7 days.

Variation

Salsa de Chicharrón: Finely chop 1 cup chicharrones into ¼-inch pieces. After the salsa is blended and while it's still warm, fold the chicharrones into the salsa. Taste and season with salt as needed.

Salsa Verde Cruda

MAKES ABOUT 4 CUPS

5 medium-large tomatillos, husked, rinsed, and quartered

1 jalapeño chile, stemmed and roughly chopped

1 serrano chile, stemmed and roughly chopped

4 scallions (white and green parts), trimmed and sliced

½ bunch of cilantro, roughly chopped (leaves and tender stems; about 1 cup)

⅓ cup fresh lime juice (2 to 3 limes)

¼ cup olive oil

½ teaspoon Morton kosher salt, plus more as needed

Special Equipment

Food processor

Many of the salsas in this chapter call for boiled, versus raw, tomatillos as a way of gradually softening their acidity and coaxing some of the umami-like properties that they—like tomatoes—can contribute to a dish. Yet, as we have seen time and time again, some privileged tacos in the top 1 percent of richness don't exactly need more. Some might say they need a bracing, citrusy reality check that levels the playing field, restores the order, and spreads the wealth—and raw tomatillos are just the measure we need to make VERY RICH tacos the best they can absolutely be! We are Fermín and Jorge, and we approve this message.

1. In a food processor, blend the tomatillos for 1 minute. Add the jalapeño, serrano, scallions, and cilantro and process for about 30 seconds or until you reach a roughly chopped consistency.
2. With the food processor running, stream in the lime juice, followed by the olive oil, and process for another 30 seconds to 1 minute, until you reach a light green color and a rustic consistency (i.e., not totally smooth, with flecks of cilantro and chile still visible).
3. Transfer to a bowl and stir in the salt. Taste and season with more salt as needed. Store in an airtight container in the fridge for 5 to 7 days.

Salsa de Chile de Árbol

MAKES ABOUT 3 CUPS

- 10 chiles de árbol, stemmed
- 3 red bell peppers, halved and stemmed
- 3 garlic cloves, peeled
- 1 teaspoon black peppercorns
- 1 teaspoon coriander seeds
- ½ cup roughly chopped cilantro stems
- 6 tablespoons neutral oil
- 1 tablespoon distilled white vinegar, plus more as needed
- ½ teaspoon Morton kosher salt, plus more as needed

Special Equipment

- Blender

What do mayonnaise and salsa de chile de árbol have in common? Answer: They are both emulsified with oil. (Golly gosh, we always knew we liked this salsa for some reason!) Anyhow, at about six times the Scovilles of jalapeños, chiles de árbol are among the spiciest we call for in this cookbook, so this salsa does lean toward the hotter side of the spectrum. Not to be forgotten, however, the red bell peppers are the figurative glass of cold milk that our palates need to mellow the burn and keep coming back for more.

1. In a large pot over high heat, bring about 10 cups of water to a boil. Carefully add the chiles de árbol, bell peppers, and garlic. Reduce the heat to medium and simmer until the bell peppers are tender and the chiles are rehydrated, 12 to 15 minutes. Reserving 1 cup of the cooking liquid, drain the vegetables and let cool for 5 minutes.
2. Meanwhile, heat a dry skillet over medium heat. Toast the peppercorns and coriander seeds, stirring frequently, until fragrant, 2 to 3 minutes. Remove from the pan to stop the cooking.
3. In a blender, combine the cooked vegetables, toasted spices, the cilantro stems, and ½ cup of the reserved cooking liquid. Blend on high speed until smooth, adding more cooking liquid as needed to achieve a smooth consistency.
4. With the blender running on medium-low speed, slowly stream in the oil to emulsify the salsa. This will create a creamy texture and brighter color.
5. Add the vinegar and salt and blend briefly to incorporate. Taste and season with more salt and vinegar as needed.
6. Transfer to a bowl to cool to room temperature. Store in an airtight container in the fridge for 5 to 7 days.

Salsa de Molcajete

MAKES 2½ TO 4 CUPS

- 4 guajillo chiles, stemmed, seeded, and veins removed
- 3 ripe Roma (plum) tomatoes
- 1 medium onion, halved
- 4 garlic cloves, peeled
- 1 serrano chile, stemmed and seeded
- ½ cup minced cilantro (leaves and tender stems)
- 1 tablespoon neutral oil
- 1 tablespoon distilled white vinegar, plus more as needed
- Kosher salt

Special Equipment

Charcoal or gas grill or comal; molcajete, food processor, or blender

How to Use a Molcajete

Salsa de molcajete is often on the savory side of salsas and among the least spicy we offer on tap at the vitamina T salsa bar. More often than not, it's the kind of salsa we might spoon directly from molcajete to mouth. It will result in pleasure no matter the application, but there is a lot to be said for using this to top something understated, even plain. We especially love it with totopos (tortilla chips) or warm tostadas with a bit of Asiento (page 255) and queso fresco, or Bean and Cheese Tamales (page 159).

1. In a medium bowl, combine the guajillo chiles and enough hot water to cover. Soak the guajillos until soft, about 10 minutes. Drain and set aside.
2. Prepare a gas or charcoal grill to medium-high heat. (Alternatively, heat a comal, griddle, or large skillet over medium-high heat on the stovetop.) Grill the tomatoes, onion, garlic, and serrano until they are charred and blistered, turning occasionally to char evenly and removing each one when done. This should take 8 to 10 minutes for the tomatoes and onion on the grill (closer to 20 to 25 on the comal) and 3 to 5 minutes for the garlic and serrano on the grill (a bit longer on the comal). Allow the grilled vegetables to cool slightly, then remove most of the tomato skins. Some charred bits of skin will add more depth of flavor to your salsa.
3. Using the tejolote (pestle) of your molcajete, grind the softened guajillo chiles until relatively smooth with a bit of texture. Add the charred onion, garlic, and serrano and mash until well incorporated. Add the charred tomatoes and mash until you get a rustic, chunky texture. Not familiar with using a molcajete? Scan the QR code for a visual. (Alternatively, use the pulse function on a food processor or blender.)
4. Stir in the cilantro, oil, and vinegar, and season to taste with salt. Adjust the consistency with a bit of water or extra vinegar as needed. Transfer the salsa to a bowl or serve right in the molcajete. Store in an airtight container in the fridge for 5 to 7 days.

Salsa Macha

MAKES 3 TO 4 CUPS

- 4 ancho chiles, stemmed and seeded
- 4 guajillo chiles, stemmed, seeded, and veins removed
- 8 chiles de árbol, stemmed and seeded
- 8 garlic cloves, peeled
- 1 cup raw sesame seeds
- ½ cup raw peanuts
- ½ cup raw pumpkin seeds
- 1 cup olive oil
- 6 tablespoons apple cider vinegar, plus more as needed
- 1 tablespoon Morton kosher salt, plus more as needed

Special Equipment

Food processor

Literally translated as "brave salsa" (a reference to the spice level of some machas, though not necessarily this one), salsa macha is a type of chile oil traditionally prepared with some combination of chiles, nuts and/or seeds, spices, and occasionally dried fruits. This version is fundamentally savory with a vinegary base note and a hint of sweetness from the ancho chiles (which we have been known to eat right out of the bag, like dried fruit). With the exception of the garlic, this salsa macha is composed of dry, shelf-stable ingredients, which should give you up to four weeks of freshness—if you can even ration it for that long.

1. Preheat the oven to 350°F.
2. Heat a dry skillet over medium heat and toast the ancho chiles, followed by the guajillo chiles, then the chiles de árbol, pressing them down occasionally until fragrant, about 2 minutes each for the ancho and guajillo chiles and 1 minute for the chiles de árbol, taking care not to burn them. Transfer the chiles to a bowl and allow them to cool for about 5 minutes.
3. In a food processor, pulse the garlic and the toasted chiles until finely chopped. Transfer to a metal bowl.
4. Spread the sesame seeds on the sheet pan and bake until toasted and golden brown, about 10 minutes, stirring every few minutes. Transfer the sesame seeds to the bowl.
5. Spread the peanuts on a sheet pan and bake until toasted, about 10 minutes, stirring every few minutes. Transfer the peanuts to the bowl.
6. Spread the pumpkin seeds on the sheet pan and bake until toasted, about 5 minutes, stirring halfway through. Transfer the pumpkin seeds to the bowl.
7. In a small saucepan, warm the olive oil over medium heat until hot but not smoking. Carefully pour the hot oil over the contents of the bowl.
8. Add the vinegar and salt and stir until combined. Taste and season with more salt and vinegar as needed.
9. Transfer the salsa macha to a clean jar or container. Let it cool to room temperature before sealing. Store in the fridge for up to 4 weeks.

Chipotle Mayo

MAKES ABOUT 3 CUPS

- 1 (7-ounce) can chipotle chiles in adobo sauce (La Morena is our pick)
- 1½ cups mayonnaise
- ¼ medium red onion, finely diced
- Juice of 2 limes (about 3 tablespoons)
- Kosher salt

Special Equipment

Food processor

We feel as passionately about mayo as Benjamin Buford "Bubba" Blue felt about shrimp in *Forrest Gump*. We can't get enough of the stuff, and for folks who know us well, they well know our belief that the evolutionary purpose of most foods is to serve at the pleasure of mayo. One of the qualities we love most about this condiment is its ability to support other condiments we enjoy, like chipotles in adobo; talk about a team player! A perfectly emulsified, foundationally fit specimen, mayo is able to catch, lift, and hold nearly anything that runs toward it, like Patrick Swayze catching Jennifer Grey in *Dirty Dancing*. Unlike that iconic sequence, though, the prep time for this number is only a handful of minutes.

In a food processor, combine the chipotles and all the adobo sauce, the mayonnaise, onion, and lime juice and puree until smooth. Season to taste with salt. Store in an airtight container in the fridge for 7 to 10 days.

Pico de Gallo

Fermín's resting energy level is the average person's pumped, and let's just say he was super-duper pumped when he shared this spectacularly subtle recipe twist on pico de gallo. Also known as salsa mexicana on account of its green (serrano), white (onion), and red (tomato) colors, this version is inspired by the same kind of pico de gallo traditionally used on the Guacamaya torta (page 63). Guacamaya pico is prepared by folding guajillo puree into trad pico's chopped ingredients; it's as simple—and as thrilling for Fermín—as that.

MAKES ABOUT 2 CUPS

- 2 guajillo chiles, stems removed
- Juice of 4 limes
- Kosher salt
- 4 medium heirloom or large Roma (plum) tomatoes, roughly diced
- 1 small white onion, finely diced
- 1 serrano chile, stemmed and thinly sliced into rounds
- ¼ cup minced cilantro (leaves and tender stems)

Special Equipment

Blender

1. In a medium bowl, combine the guajillo chiles and enough hot water to cover. Soak the guajillos until soft, about 15 minutes. Drain the chiles.
2. In a blender, combine the guajillos and the lime juice and blend until smooth. Season to taste with salt.
3. In a medium bowl, combine the tomatoes, onion, serrano, and cilantro. Stir in the blended guajillo chiles and season to taste with salt. Store in an airtight container in the fridge for 5 to 7 days.

Asiento

MAKES ABOUT 3 CUPS

1½ pounds pork fatback, cut into 1-inch cubes

1 pound boneless pork shoulder, cut into ¼-inch cubes

2 bay leaves

1 head of garlic, halved horizontally

Special Equipment

Food processor

Asiento and masa go together like butter and baguettes, but asiento is better and definitely not butter; technically, it's rendered pork fat flecked with crispy pork bits. Several recipes in this cookbook call for asiento, but you also can't go wrong with a smear of it on any one of your favorite masa-based dishes, especially warm tortillas. A fine-mesh strainer such as a chinois will be your friend here, but lining a colander with cheesecloth can work in a pinch.

1. In a 6-quart soup pot over medium-low heat, add the pork fatback, pork shoulder, bay leaves, and garlic. Cook until the pork fat has liquefied and the pork shoulder has crisped up, about 2½ hours.
2. Discard the bay leaves and garlic. Using a chinois or large fine-mesh sieve set over a bowl or pot, carefully strain the solids from the liquid. Reserve both the solids and the liquid fat. Place the fat in the fridge to cool.
3. In a food processor, blitz the cooked solids until smooth. Mix the cooked paste into the cooled fat. Store in an airtight container in the fridge for up to 1 week.

Guacamole

As is true with superior salsas, the best-testing guacamole is prepared in a molcajete. By mashing, kneading, and extracting the essential oils in each core ingredient, a basalt molcajete magically unlocks layers of flavor that would otherwise lie dormant in chopped form. You can always throw in additional chopped components for some textural contrast after your mash sesh is over—we certainly do—but they will now be supporting players to your Oscar-winning ensemble cast.

1. Using the tejolote (pestle) of your molcajete, grind a coarse paste of the onion, chile, salt, and half the cilantro. The salt acts as an abrasive, assisting as you grind. Not familiar with using a molcajete? Scan the QR code for a visual.
2. Scoop the avocado flesh into the molcajete. Mix well with the paste and add the remaining cilantro, giving it a rough mash. Season to taste with lime juice and salt.

Vitamina T(ip)

If you like the texture of diced onion in your guac, mash only half of the onion in the molcajete and reserve the remainder to mix in at the end.

MAKES ABOUT 2 CUPS

3 tablespoons diced onion (see Tip)

1 tablespoon minced serrano chile or jalapeño chile, including seeds (or more, depending on heat tolerance)

1 teaspoon Morton kosher salt, plus more as needed

¼ cup minced cilantro

3 large avocados, halved

Juice of 1 or 2 limes

Special Equipment

Molcajete

How to Use a Molcajete

Escabeche

MAKES 2 TO 3 QUARTS

- 6 cups distilled white vinegar
- ½ cup sugar
- 3 tablespoons Morton kosher salt
- Olive oil
- 6 large jalapeño chiles, stemmed and halved lengthwise
- 1½ medium onions, sliced (about 3 cups)
- 2 medium carrots, sliced into ¼-inch-thick rounds (about 3 cups)
- ½ small head of cauliflower, trimmed and broken into florets (about 3 cups)
- 1 tablespoon dried Mexican oregano
- 2 teaspoons freshly ground black pepper

The Spanish brought their well-established tradition of pickling fish on some of their earliest voyages to Mexico, which in turn led to Mexicans pickling local ingredients like chiles—and the rest is history. Today, this condiment is virtually inseparable from tortas, as it brings the oft-rich elements of the sandwiches into glorious equilibrium—but don't let that hold you back from working it into or alongside your favorite savory foods. Jalapeños are first on this easy-breezy production's call sheet, but don't sleep on the onions, carrots, and cauli florets.

1. In a medium saucepan, combine the vinegar, sugar, and salt, and bring to a boil over medium-high heat.
2. Meanwhile, heat a cast-iron skillet over medium heat and add just enough oil to coat the bottom of the pan. Add the jalapeños, stirring constantly so they get some color but don't soften, no more than 3 minutes. Transfer to a medium bowl and keep near the stove.
3. In the skillet, repeat the same process with the onions, cooking them to give some color, which should take about half as long as the jalapeños. Transfer to the bowl.
4. Follow the same process with the carrots, cooking them until they have a bit of color but are not softened. Transfer to the bowl.
5. Repeat with the cauliflower.
6. Add the oregano and pepper to the bowl and mix by hand or with a spoon until the seasoning is evenly distributed.
7. Place the cooked vegetables in a large glass container or multiple smaller containers and pour the hot vinegar brine over to cover. Let cool, then seal with a lid. Store in the fridge for at least 1 day and up to 1 month.

Habanero-Pickled Onions

MAKES ABOUT 4 CUPS

- 3 large red onions, thinly sliced
- 3 fresh habanero chiles, stemmed and thinly sliced (seeds removed depending on heat tolerance)
- 1 teaspoon ground coriander
- 1 teaspoon dried Mexican oregano
- 1 teaspoon Morton kosher salt
- ½ teaspoon freshly ground black pepper
- 1 cup distilled white vinegar
- 1 cup apple cider vinegar

When all is said and done, these pickled onions should serve as a crunchy, acidic foil for fiery foods. For the spice-averse, note that the spices and pickling process will ultimately mellow the habaneros—we promise! Don't forget to use Morton kosher salt for the precise salt measurement here, as not all salts are created equal (see page 20).

1. In a large glass jar (or 2 or 3, depending on their size), combine the red onions, habaneros, coriander, oregano, salt, and pepper.
2. In a small saucepan, combine both vinegars and bring to a boil over medium-high heat. Pour the hot vinegars over the mixture in the jar(s) to cover the ingredients.
3. Allow the onions to cool to room temperature. Once cooled, seal with a lid and store in the fridge for up to 4 weeks.

Chamoy

While chamoy holds a special place in the canon of Mexican condiment offerings, we're not especially fond of the store-bought version, with its pervasive artificial coloring and cloying candy flavor. Homemade chamoy, however, is a different story. Chamoy captures the full canon of Mexican flavors; a drizzle will activate your sweet, salty, spicy, and sour flavor receptors like Pop Rocks. You'll find this more balanced version to be a lot less runny in consistency than store-bought, so a little bit should go a long(er) way. If it's your first time working with citric acid, don't let it intimidate you; it is a weak acid in powder form that occurs naturally in citrus fruits like lemons and limes. While optional, it gives an extra sour-candy acidic punch.

MAKES 2½ TO 3 CUPS

- ½ cup sugar
- ½ cup (4 ounces) dried apricots
- ¼ cup (2 ounces) golden raisins
- ¼ cup (2 ounces) dried hibiscus
- 4 guajillo chiles, stemmed, seeded, and veins removed
- 4 piquín chiles
- ½ cup distilled white vinegar
- 2 teaspoons Morton kosher salt, plus more as needed
- 1 teaspoon citric acid (optional)

Special Equipment

Blender (preferably high-powered, such as Vitamix)

1. In a medium pot over medium-low heat, combine about 4 cups of water, the sugar, apricots, raisins, hibiscus, and the chiles, and cook at a low simmer until the liquid is reduced and the fruit is soft, 30 minutes.
2. Working in 2 batches, transfer the cooked ingredients and liquid to a blender and blend until smooth, streaming in half of the vinegar for each batch to loosen—you're looking for a slightly thick, syrupy consistency. (If your blender isn't high-powered, you may want to strain the mixture for a smooth texture.) When both batches are fully blended, transfer to a bowl and mix in the salt and citric acid (if using). Taste and season with more salt as needed. Store in an airtight container in the fridge for up to 4 weeks.

Jorge's Acknowledgments

To Fermín, the suadero to this corn tortilla, it remains an absolute joy working with you on all things, especially this book, friend. Thank you for your presence, spirit, and friendship throughout this journey.

To Allegra, for manifesting this cookbook in Chicago and becoming such an integral part of it, after all. Your relentless standards and passion made this project all the better for it.

To Jeni and Dylan, for capturing the essence of VT so vividly; Daniel for being the glue that held our many creative schemes together; Nidia for bringing a slice of Omar to VT; Carlos and Dani for bringing these recipes to life; Alex for starting us off on the right foot; and Kristina, for your early testing and thoughtful feedback.

To Andrianna, for championing another one. Francis, for seeing and trusting the vision; this was a dream come true for me. Susan, for being this project's steady hand each step of the way. Darian, for your BTS hustle. Robert, you are a true magician.

To the entire Masienda team, for your collective support before, during, and after this book's production—each of you. I am forever grateful. Hallie, for planting the seeds for this project, and Danielle, for always keeping it on the rails.

To all of my family and friends, especially my G-girls—Julia, Senna, Luisa (and Ru)—I love you.

Fermín's Acknowledgments

This book is dedicated to every taquero, taquera, tortero, tamalera, mayora, and cocinero who wakes up every day to do what they love and serve people delicious food made to order with dignity and pride. For every Mexican who is proud of being Mexican near and far away from our country, this one is for us.

Cooking is easy—managing and running restaurants is a bit more complicated. To my team and partners at our restaurants, for allowing me to have the flexibility to work on this dream project, gracias, you know exactly who you are.

Jorge, for not only trusting me in coming up with over a hundred recipes that mostly started with the letter T, but for putting together an incredible group of individuals who share the same passion for Mexico, tacos, and all things masa, thank you.

Familia—Mamá, Tania—although I didn't get any cooking skills or tips from either of y'all, I wouldn't be who I am without you, and maybe that was for the best, las amo.

To Jacqueline, for being there, but most importantly, for allowing me to be me and letting me be so I can do the things I love, like this book, merci beaucoup.

Glossary

JALE POR ABAJO
CONTENIDO 250 SERVILLETAS
HECHO CON 90% a 100% DE FIBRAS RECICLADAS
Servilleta Interdoblada
Práctica Bolsa Despachador para usar colgada.
Abrir aquí
Kimberly-Clark PROFESSIONAL
Servilletas

adobada: Spanish for "marinated"; generally used to describe meat that has been cooked in an adobo sauce consisting of chiles, spices, and vinegar.

ahogada: Spanish for "drowned," as in "drowned in salsa."

alambre: A medley of meat, onions, peppers, and bacon, served with tortillas on the side for DIY tacos.

a la talla: Means "to size"; refers specifically to a whole butterflied fish grilled over an open flame.

asada: Spanish for "grilled," referring both to the adjective and the noun denoting a grill cookout.

asiento: Derived from the Spanish verb asentar (to settle), the Oaxacan name for a type of lard commonly used for masa-based dishes like tlayudas and memelas. It specifically refers to the settled fat that remains after rendering, frying, and cooling pork, most often chicharrón (pork rind).

atole: A warm masa-based beverage that is often consumed with tamales.

barbacoa: The Mesoamerican dish consisting of goat or lamb wrapped in maguey leaves and slow-cooked underground or in a clay oven.

birria: A relative of barbacoa, birria is essentially braised, shredded meat accompanied with a spicy beef broth (known as consomé) and tortillas.

bistec: Beef steak.

bolillo: A bun used for tortas; somewhere between a bánh mi–style baguette and a hoagie roll.

buñuelo: A sweet, tortilla-like fritter.

cacahuazintle: A breed of corn with large kernels, regionally prized for its application in pozole, esquites, and tamales.

cachetada: Spanish for "slap," and the name for a taco consisting of thinly sliced rib eye, cheese, and sautéed onions—which happens to slap.

cal: Also known as slaked lime, cal is the Spanish colloquial word referring to either calcium oxide or calcium hydroxide, used primarily for nixtamalization.

camote: Spanish for sweet potato. In Mexico City, a dying breed of street vendor is the camotero, who sells sweet potatoes roasted in a wood-fired cart, his presence announced by the shrill whistle of steam being released.

canasta: Spanish for "basket," as in tacos de canasta, or tacos steamed in a basket.

canela: Spanish for "cinnamon," specifically Ceylon cinnamon.

carne apache: Raw beef "cooked" in citrus, much like a ceviche.

carne deshebrada: Shredded or pulled beef.

carne seca: "Dried meat"; a thin Mexican-style beef jerky.

carnitas: Meat, typically pork, that has been slow-cooked in its own fat.

cecina: Salted, dried meat (usually pork or beef).

cemita: Refers to both the sesame-coated, challah-like sandwich bun and the Pueblan torta served on the bun of the same name, consisting of breaded beef, quesillo, avocado, onion, and pápalo.

chamoy: A sweet-sour-spicy Mexican condiment that can be found in sauce, paste, or powder form.

champurrado: A chocolate- and spice-infused atole.

charro: A Mexican cowboy.

Cheesy Gordita Crunch: The Taco Bell creation consisting of a crunchy hard-shell (corn) taco filled with ground beef, lettuce, Cheddar cheese, and spicy ranch, wrapped in a thick, cheesy flour tortilla.

chicharrón: Any type of pork rind, whether it be puffy, crunchy, pressed, or merely referential (i.e., chicharrón de harina, or flour).

chilaquiles: A classic breakfast dish consisting of fried tortilla chips cooked in salsa and topped with shaved onions, cheese, crema, and (optional) fried egg or shredded chicken.

chiquihuite: A woven tortilla basket/holder.

chorizera: Also known as a discada, a metal comal (griddle or pan) with a raised convex center and circular trough that runs around its circumference.

cochinita pibil: Traditional Yucatecan dish consisting of pork marinated in achiote that is slow-cooked in an underground pit (pib).

comal: A flat griddle made of earthenware or metal.

comida: Spanish for "food" or "meal," in addition to being the term for the largest meal of the day, usually eaten around lunchtime or late afternoon.

concha: Spanish for "shell"; named for a brioche-like roll with a sweet striated topping that bears resemblance to a shell.

consomé: A broth typically served alongside dishes like barbacoa or birria.

costra: Spanish for "crust," usually in the form of griddled caramelized cheese. It is sometimes used as a replacement for a tortilla in a taco, but more often appears as a textural addition that adheres to the inside or outside of the tortilla.

cruda: Spanish for "raw," and a colloquial term for hungover.

cubana: A Mexican torta consisting of pork carnitas, steak milanesa, sausage, Manchego cheese, and so much more.

cubano: Cuban sándwich consisting of lechón (roast pork), ham, Swiss cheese, pickles, and yellow mustard.

doradita: Golden, caramelized, crispy.

dorilocos: A Mexican street snack that's even wilder than its cousin tostilocos, consisting of Doritos, grated carrot, jicama, cucumber, pickled pork rinds, "Japanese" peanuts, chamoy, Valentina hot sauce, lime, candied chile powder (a.k.a. Miguelito) or Tajín, all served straight out of the Doritos bag.

Edomae sushi: An old-school style of sushi originating in nineteenth-century Tokyo that utilizes traditional techniques for preserving and developing the flavor and textures of fresh seafood.

Electrolit: A Mexican-made electrolyte beverage; think something between Pedialyte, Gatorade, and a flat Jarritos.

elote: Corn on the cob loaded with some combination of mayo, lime, chile powder, and crumbled cheese; may also generally refer to fresh corn.

enchiladas: A dish consisting of a corn tortilla wrapped around a filling. There are many regional variations, some featuring salsa mixed in to the tortilla masa, some in which tortillas are dipped in salsa, and some in which the rolled tortillas are covered in salsa. Depending on the region, it may be baked into a casserole format.

enchiladas suizas: "Swiss"-style enchiladas that have heavy cream, crema, or cream cheese mixed into the salsa, so named for the abundance of dairy in Swiss cuisine.

epazote: A culinary and medicinal leafy herb with black pepper notes, used throughout Mexican cooking, especially in beans, where it is thought to have gas-relieving properties.

escabeche: In Mexico, a mixture of conserved, pickled vegetables in vinegar.

escamoles: Ant larvae, a seasonal Mexican delicacy.

esquites: A quintessential Mexican street snack made of boiled corn kernels topped with some combination of mayo, lime, chile powder, and crumbled cheese.

fam bam: Also known as familia, or family meal, the pre-service meal shared by front- and back-of-house team members at a restaurant.

flauta: A rolled, deep-fried taco.

fonda: A small, casual restaurant or eatery, often found in markets and specializing in comida corrida—a homey, multicourse, Mexican take on fast food, or food in a hurry.

FUD: Fine, Unique, and Delicious, FUD is a Mexican American brand of processed deli meats and cheese products, owned by parent company Sigma Alimentos.

gaonera: Thinly sliced beef tenderloin.

garnacha: Also known as a sope, a thin masa pancake with an outer ridge.

guacamaya: Spanish for "macaw" and the name for the classic torta filled with chicharrones, pickled pork rinds, salsa, lime mayo, and pico de gallo.

guajolota: A tamal-filled torta, and the Nahuatl-derived name for a female turkey.

guisado: A braise or stew. Tacos de guisados refers to the category of tacos made from such (assorted) braises.

hoja: A leaf or husk.

hoja de aguacate: Avocado leaf, the anise-flavored addition often made to beans, stews, and salsas.

hoja santa: Translated as "sacred leaf," a culinary herb with an anise-like flavor, also known as root beer plant.

huarache: A masa-based dish in the shape of the eponymous woven leather sandal commonly worn throughout Mexico.

huitlacoche: Corn smut, also known as cuitlacoche; a fungus prized for its truffle-like flavor that grows on maize and causes kernels to turn gray and swell in size.

itacate: Colloquial word of Nahuatl origin used to describe food provisions for a journey (i.e., to-go food). Itacate also happens to be a tetela-like, triangular, stuffed masa dish that is a popular street food in Tepoztlán, Mexico.

Jeff: Kitchen colloquialism for "chef," immortalized, though not conceived, by *The Bear.*

John Bradshaw: An iconic leader of the self-help movement who championed the concept of reclaiming the inner child within each of us.

laminada: Spanish for "laminated" or "sheeted," referring in *Vitamina T* to thinly sliced, layered meat, such as al pastor.

laminated pastries: Baked goods, such as croissants, featuring many thin layers of dough and butter, produced through repeated folding and sheeting.

lengua: Tongue, typically of beef.

lonche: A cake; also known as a torta.

longaniza: A type of sausage made of minced (versus ground) meat.

machaca: Finely shredded carne seca; a meat floss.

maciza: A leaner cut of meat, such as shoulder meat, typically referenced in relation to pork carnitas.

Maggi: The umami condiment of champions, found in kitchens and on restaurant tables throughout Mexico.

manteca: Lard.

masa: The Spanish word for "dough." In the context of this book, it refers to a dough originating in Mesoamerican cuisine, made from ground corn that has been cooked and steeped in an alkaline solution.

masa harina: Spanish for "masa flour," referring to dehydrated ground masa.

masa preparada: A prepared masa for tamales, to which broth, lard, baking powder, and seasoning have already been added.

memela: A thick tortilla with subtle indentations for retaining salsas and toppings; a textured masa pancake.

Mesoamerican: Of or pertaining to the historic region extending from modern-day Mexico to Costa Rica.

milanesa: "Milanese" style, referring to a breaded and pan-fried protein or vegetable, such as chicken, beef cutlets, or eggplant.

milpa: The Mesoamerican word referring to both a cornfield and the complementary cultivation of corn, beans, and squash (a.k.a. the "three sisters" of agriculture).

molcajete: A mortar and pestle, traditionally made of basalt.

mulita: A taco sandwich made of meat and cheese assembled between two corn tortillas.

nata: Boiled, unpasteurized milk that is similar in flavor and texture to clotted cream and mascarpone.

nixtamalization: Derived from the Nahuatl words nextli (ash) and tamalli (unformed corn dough or tamal), the Mesoamerican process of cooking and steeping corn (though other ingredients may also apply) in an alkaline solution.

"no manches": An expression of surprise or disbelief, meaning "no way!". A perfect example of the art of albur, or Mexican wordplay/double entendre. Similar to the way Americans might use "sugar" to express a more vulgar term, "no manches" (literally meaning "don't stain") is the more polite way to express disbelief, a play on the more vulgar "no mames" (literally translated as "don't suck").

nopal: Cactus paddle.

norteño: Of or relating to northern Mexico.

olla: A pot, traditionally made of clay.

pambazo: A torta, the Mexico City version of which features chorizo with potato between two guajillo-soaked buns.

pan de elote: Mexican equivalent of corn bread.

pápalo: A leafy herb with a flavor reminiscent of cilantro but stronger.

pepitas: Pumpkin seeds.

pescadilla: Also known as a sope, or thick masa pancake with a ridge.

picadillo: Stewed ground beef.

pipián: A type of stew widely associated with mole verde (green mole).

poblana: Of or relating to Puebla.

puesto: Any stall, stand, or spot where food is served.

qué onda: Mexican slang for "What's up?"

quesabirria: A quesadilla-birria taco mash-up that originated in Tijuana.

quesadilla: A corn tortilla, folded in half and filled with ingredients that may or may not include cheese (if you're in Mexico City), then fried or cooked on a comal or in a pan.

quesillo: A low-moisture, stringy melting cheese (a.k.a. queso Oaxaca) similar to mozzarella.

queso asadero: A high-protein, low-moisture Mexican grilling cheese, comparable to halloumi.

rajas: "Strips," typically cut from roasted chiles, most often chile poblanos.

raspadas: An iconic style of tostada made in the Mexican state of Jalisco that has a rough, craggy surface texture.

regiomontana: Of or relating to the Mexican city of Monterrey.

requesón: A salty, spreadable Mexican cheese, similar in profile to ricotta.

salpicón: A marinated meat "salad."

salsa macha: A type of chile oil traditionally prepared with some combination of chiles, nuts and/or seeds, spices, and occasionally dried fruits.

sangrita: Translated as "little blood," a non-alcoholic tequila chaser made with some combination of tomato juice, orange juice, lime juice, and hot sauce.

sazón: Seasoning, flavor, the good stuff.

sikil pak: A hearty Yucatecan salsa made of pepitas, with a texture akin to hummus.

sopa seca de natas: A casserole-ish dish originating in Guadalajara, consisting of layered crepes with a cream-infused tomato sauce and shredded chicken.

sope: Thick masa pancake with a raised outer ridge meant for retaining toppings.

suadero: Beef confit, traditionally of the rose meat (a.k.a. navel plate) cut. It is also the name of Fermín's future first child.

surtido: An assortment or mix, specifically a combination of meat cuts, including offal, used for carnitas.

taco al vapor: Steamed taco.

taco dorado: A "golden taco," either folded or rolled, then fried.

Tajín: The official brand and proprietary eponym for the seasoning blend of chile, lime, and sea salt.

tamal: A wrapped, often steamed, masa cake.

tamalada: A tamal-making party.

tamalera: A pot used for steaming tamales.

taquero/a: A professional taco slinger.

tasajo: Spanish for "piece of meat," literally. In Mexico, tasajo most often refers to salted and air-dried meat, typically beef.

tatemada: Charred, burnt, and/or blistered.

telera: Oblong ciabatta-like rolls used for tortas, with two lengthwise indentations running along the top.

ternt: American slang for "turned," inspired by the debut solo album, *Rappa Ternt Sanga,* by rapper/singer T-Pain.

tetela: Masa that has been stuffed with a filling and folded into a neat, triangular empanada form, somewhat reminiscent of a crepe.

tianguis: An open-air, makeshift market.

tinga: Originating from the Nahuatl word tingatl, which means "to tear," tinga is composed of torn or shredded meat, commonly chicken, though pork is believed to be the truest of the tinga OGs.

tlacoyo: Oval-shaped, stuffed masa turnover.

tlayuda: Large-format tortilla, often upwards of 13 inches in diameter, hailing from the state of Oaxaca.

torta: Spanish for "cake," a Mexican sandwich.

tortería: A torta shop/restaurant; a torta-tessen.

tortero/a: A torta artist.

tortilla blanda: A soft tortilla.

tortillería: A tortilla bakery.

tostada: A crispy, "toasted" tortilla that can be baked, fried, or pan-toasted.

tostilocos: A Mexican street snack roughly consisting of Tostitos, grated carrot, jicama, cucumber, pickled pork rinds, "Japanese" peanuts, chamoy, Valentina hot sauce, lime, candied chile powder (a.k.a. Miguelito) or Tajín, all served straight out of the Tostitos bag.

totopos: Tortilla chips.

tripas: Tripe (preferably the small intestine).

trompo: A vertically assembled spit of slow-roasting meat, such as pork al pastor.

verdolagas: Purslane, an edible succulent with a lemony flavor profile.

vitamina T: An affectionate, pseudoscientific, colloquial 1990s term for the delicious category of Mexican street foods beginning with the letter *T,* such as tamales, tortas, tacos, tlacoyos, tlayudas . . .

Index

Clarkson Potter/Publishers
An imprint of the Crown Publishing Group
A division of Penguin Random House LLC
1745 Broadway
New York, NY 10019
clarksonpotter.com
penguinrandomhouse.com

Library of Congress Cataloging-in-Publication Data
Names: Gaviria, Jorge author | Núñez, Fermín author | Ho, Dylan James photographer | Afuso, Jeni photographer Title: Vitamina T : Your Daily Dose of Tacos, Tortas, Tamales, and More Mexican Street Food Classics / Jorge Gaviria and Fermín Núñez; photographs by Jeni Afuso and Dylan James Ho.
Description: New York: Clarkson Potter/Publishers, [2026] | Includes index. Identifiers: LCCN 2025010373 (print) | LCCN 2025010374 (ebook) | ISBN 9780593800379 hardcover | ISBN 9780593800386 ebook Subjects: LCSH: Cooking, Mexican | LCGFT: Cookbooks Classification: LCC TX716.M4 G385 2026 (print) | LCC TX716.M4 (ebook) | DDC 641.5972—dc23/eng/20250319
LC record available at https://lccn.loc.gov/2025010373
LC ebook record available at https://lccn.loc.gov/2025010374

ISBN 978-0-593-80037-9
Ebook ISBN 978-0-593-80038-6

Editors: Francis Lam and Susan Roxborough
Assistant editor: Darian Keels
Designer: Robert Diaz
Photographers: Jeni Afuso and Dylan James Ho
Location scout: Alex Roa
Production editor: Sohayla Farman
Production designer: Christina Self
Production: Kim Tyner
Compositors: Merri Ann Morrell, Nick Patton, and Hannah Hunt
Recipe editor: Allegra Ben-Amotz
Photoshoot director: Daniel Klein
Food stylist assistant: Carlos Garcia de la Cabada
Prop stylist: Nidia Cueva
Recipe developers: Ale Kuri and Derrick Flynn
Copyeditor: Carole Berglie
Proofreaders: Rachel Markowitz, Erica Rose, Allie Kiekhofer, and Christina Caruccio
Indexer: Ken DellaPenta
Publicists: Felix Cruz and David Hawk
Marketer: Joey Lozada

Manufactured in Malaysia

10 9 8 7 6 5 4 3 2 1

First Edition

The authorized representative in the EU for product safety and compliance is Penguin Random House Ireland, Morrison Chambers, 32 Nassau Street, Dublin D02 YH68, Ireland, https://eu-contact.penguin.ie.

Jorge Gaviria is the James Beard Award–winning founder of Masienda and the bestselling author of *MASA: Techniques, Recipes, and Reflections on a Timeless Staple*. Prior to founding Masienda, he was an educator, a pig herder, and line cook. He has trained at Danny Meyer's Union Square Hospitality Group and Blue Hill at Stone Barns.

A native of Torreón, Mexico, **Fermín Núñez** is the chef and co-owner of the award-winning restaurants Suerte, Este, and Bar Toti in Austin, Texas. Núñez has been named among *Food & Wine*'s Best New Chefs and Eater Austin's Chef of the Year. He has been featured on Food Network and Netflix's *Taco Chronicles* as well as in *The Wall Street Journal*, *The New York Times*, and *Texas Monthly*.

Allegra Ben-Amotz is a food writer, an editor, and a home cook who lives with her family in Los Angeles. Her writing has appeared in *The Washington Post*, *The Wall Street Journal*, *New York Magazine*, *Cherry Bombe*, and more. She's also the marketing director at Masienda.

Clarkson Potter/Publishers
New York
clarksonpotter.com

Cover design: Robert Diaz
Cover photograph: Jeni Afuso and Dylan James Ho

ATECA